DEVELOPME ... TO DIVISION 1

STRENGTH & CONDITIONING
FOR THE VOLLEYBALL ATHLETE

MISSY MITCHELL-MCBETH

DEVELOPMENTAL TO DIVISION I: STRENGTH AND CONDITIONING FOR THE VOLLEYBALL ATHLETE

Copyright © 2024 by
MISSY MITCHELL-MCBETH, MSEd, SCCC, CSCS, USAW

ISBN: 9798326593269

To learn more about Missy Mitchell-McBeth, visit **MissyMitchellMcBeth.com**

"Getting results is about relentless adherence to fundamentals, not fluff. Missy not only understands this, she has saturated every page with pragmatic advice that will help coaches of all ages and experience levels.

This book isn't just a resource, it's a compass that will ensure neither you, nor the athletes you serve will head down the wrong path."

– Brett Bartholomew
Best-selling author of Conscious Coaching,
Founder of ArtOfCoaching.com

"Coach Mitchell-McBeth brings a real-world, practical approach to the necessary function of strength and conditioning in a volleyball program. Athletes on teams I coached had the benefit of her expertise and in-depth background and her work was critical to the success of our program. It was refreshing to work with a strength and conditioning coach who kept the whole athlete in mind.

This book is a must-read for every volleyball coach, regardless of experience. A solid, well-thought-out strength and conditioning program is a necessary part of every successful program and it can set you apart from the competition. Coach Mitchell-McBeth's book will give coaches the knowledge they need to create a complete program; and when coaches grow their knowledge in all phases of training, they become better leaders for their athletes.

I am so thankful that Coach Mitchell-McBeth is sharing her expertise and helping other coaches grow- it's truly a needed book in this time of overtraining and piecemealed strength and conditioning programs."

– Libby Pacheco

COO Texas High School Coaches' Association Education Foundation, Former Head Volleyball Coach - Byron Nelson High School

---

"Coach Missy Mitchell-McBeth is one the best strength and conditioning minds in the country. She has a vast amount of experience and knowledge in the sport of volleyball and is methodical in her approach to training. She has a way of breaking down movements in a way that other coaches understand but more importantly in a way that athletes of any age can understand.

There is a reason for everything she does, and her training programs are scaffolded in a way that focuses on developing the total athlete by progressing movements from the ground up. For example, her squat progression starts athletes with the countermovement squat then progresses to goblet squats then to hands free barbell squats before barbell front squatting with load. Not only does this teach athletes how to squat properly, it also allows them to build confidence in their movements. I still use her coaching cues for squatting along with other movements to this day.

As a former volleyball player herself, Coach Mitchell-McBeth has a complete understanding of the demands of the sport and is able to demonstrate that effectively in her training. She also understands the needs of athletes who participate in a sport year round. One of the biggest improvements I have made as a sport coach is to improve my knowledge of strength & conditioning and she has been a big part of that. My athletes are better because of her. They are not just volleyball players. They are athletes and she deserves credit for helping us to become a championship program."

– Josh McKinney
Head Volleyball Coach - Colleyville High School (2022 5A State Champions),
Head Volleyball Coach - Texas Advantage Volleyball Club
(2023 National Champion)

"If you want to be the best in your role as a volleyball coach, this is a must read. End of Story. This book is relatable, actionable, and will allow your athletes to improve.

Missy was my strength and conditioning coach at TCU, for not only volleyball but for golf as well. She understands the female body, she knows how to train for performance, and she also has firsthand seen the impact of what overtraining looks like in youth sports. Her work to provide you with a plan that allows your athletes to perform their best is some of her best work to date."

– Alexia Heist
TCU Volleyball 2012-2016

MISSY MITCHELL - MCBETH
S P O R T S   P E R F O R M A N C E

**Scan the QR Code or visit
MissyMitchellMcBeth.com/D2D1-Bonus
to access corresponding videos and
other exclusive resources:**

CONTENTS

FOREWORD

While my title is currently Director of Human Performance at TCU, my real association with Developmental to Division I is that Coach McBeth and I have been longtime colleagues, and more importantly friends.

Our journey together began when she accepted an internship with TCU Strength and Conditioning in 2009 as a young eager coach and has grown since that day. Throughout our time together, I have witnessed firsthand Missy's growth as a coach into one of the best in the performance industry. Missy's unwavering commitment to knowledge and understanding in our field has not only earned my respect but has also enriched my career as a performance coach. There are few coaches out there that I would entrust my children's developmental path...Missy is one of them.

She has been somebody that has constantly challenged me to grow as a coach. I have often turned to her for guidance, knowing she would be able to offer insight into any situation I have encountered. Having access to her thoughts and her overall vision of a comprehensive training program is invaluable.

As a strength and conditioning coach, I understand the critical role that any performance program can play in the success, as well as the downfall of athletes. Middle school and high school weight rooms often leave much to be desired when it comes to a comprehensive strength and conditioning program. Restrictions on time, budgets, properly certified staff, etc. can all play a role in the lack of development. Often, sport coaches and parents are left to fill the developmental gaps with little to guide them.

With Developmental to Division I, there is a starting point for any athlete. This book is a comprehensive guide designed specifically for volleyball coaches who also serve as their team's strength and conditioning coach. But it's more than just a manual on lifting weights and running drills. It's a roadmap for transforming young athletes from developmental players to Division I contenders.

Even for seasoned strength coaches, "Developmental to Division I" provides the tools, knowledge, and pathway you need to take your players' physical abilities to the next level.

But it's not just coaches who will benefit from this book. Parents of volleyball players will gain valuable insights into the importance of strength training for their children's athletic development.

And for the players themselves, "Developmental to Division I" serves as a blueprint for achieving their goals on the court and beyond.

Whether you're looking to fine-tune your existing training program or starting from scratch, "Developmental to Division I" is your ultimate guide to unlocking the full potential of your volleyball athletes.

What you're about to read will help take you and/or your athletes down a path of success that you won't regret. It's an honor to introduce Coach McBeth's life work, that already has, and will continue to change athlete's lives for the better!

– Zach Dechant
Director of Human Performance, TCU
Mentor, colleagues, and most of all, friends

For my Mother, who demonstrates true strength.

PREFACE

Devastation. That's how my volleyball career started.

It was 1992 and club volleyball wasn't yet a thing in the North Texas town where I grew up. Even if it were, my family couldn't have afforded it. As a result, the entire sport of volleyball was relegated to a single week of games, which were held at my elementary school at lunchtime. With only one outside court available, tryouts determined which three boys and which three girls were the best choices for the 5th grade team.

These tryouts were based on one element of the game: serving accuracy. Best out of 10.

As I waited in line, I watched my classmates shank serve after serve wide of the court or into the net. Determined to not fall prey to the same fate, I began to formulate a strategy. I zeroed in on the old, fraying net. Suspended between two metal poles that were held upright by a pair of cement-filled tires, it sagged and dipped in the middle. A master tactician in the making, my plan of attack was simple: serve over the low spot in the net.

When my turn came up, I collected the ball and stepped confidently to the line. Despite having never held a volleyball in my hands before that moment, the prospect of failure never entered my mind. With four years of soccer under my belt and a foolproof serving strategy, I was the pinnacle of athletic preparedness.

Even after shanking my first three serves into the neighboring field, I reined it in and finished with an astonishing 6 out of 10 serves over the net and in bounds. I had secured a spot in the top 3, or so I thought, and could already feel the excitement of playing in next week's games! I marched triumphantly away from the service line knowing that only one girl remained, and she had no interest whatsoever in playing volleyball. Unfortunately, what Joanna lacked in love for the sport she more than made up for in serving capability. As her 7th serve sailed over the net and landed in bounds, my 5th grade volleyball career ended in tragedy.

For reasons I still don't understand, I didn't let failure deter me. Instead, I decided at that moment that volleyball was my new favorite sport, and I would play it *forever*.

And I have.

A year later, armed with improved serving accuracy, I made the 6th grade PE team. When athletics were an option in the 7th grade, I made that team as well. I played high school volleyball, NAIA volleyball, and as an adult I still play beach volleyball every chance I get.

All of which I did as an undersized, mediocre athlete. Not exactly the best recipe for success, but I deeply loved volleyball–and still do. I love the feeling of theft that the sport provides. Stealing an opponent's joy as their attack ricochets off the block and straight into the floor. Robbing them by digging the ball they just crushed. Removing all hope as the setter dumps into open court, the ultimate blindside.

This passion for the sport, combined with needing to improve my own athletic limitations, led me to the field of strength and conditioning. In the early stages of this journey, my interest in training was self-serving. I was trying to improve *my* strength, *my* vertical jump, and *my* volleyball game.

Fast forward to 2004 and I'm a high school volleyball coach in Copperas Cove, Texas. Due to my interest in strength and conditioning, I was placed in charge of the off-season weight room. Shockingly, despite tens of hours of reading dot-com articles about S&C, I found myself underprepared to apply this "knowledge" to large groups of beginner athletes.

After a few failed attempts to do it on my own, I sought guidance from the person who became my mentor: Reb Brock. Reb was the strength and conditioning coach and defensive coordinator at Copperas Cove High School and was kind enough to invest time in a first year volleyball coach. Through his teaching, I learned safe and effective ways to better prepare volleyball athletes to be successful on the court. I also discovered that becoming a strength and conditioning coach full-time was the next evolution of my volleyball career. I loved everything about strength and conditioning. Mirroring an athlete's excitement when they caught a hang power clean for the first time. Smiling alongside them as they flexed their hard-earned muscles after finishing a set. Watching as they grew more confident in the weight room and on the court. My previous interest in my own physical development had shifted to an interest in the development of others.

Four years later, I left my position as a high school volleyball coach to pursue strength and conditioning full-time. First at TCU, where I worked with Women's Indoor Volleyball, Women's Basketball, and Women's Golf for seven years. Next at Byron Nelson High School, where I trained all sports, including the 2019 Texas 6A State Champion and USA Today #1 ranked volleyball program. Then, while writing this, in the private sector with Fieldhouse Volleyball Club in the Dallas Fort Worth Metro area and as a consultant for multiple high school volleyball programs.

The contents of this book are the product of almost 20 years of trial and error, success and failure, organized and simplified so that you don't have to experiment to find what works. I've done that for you.

This book is for the volleyball coaches out there who don't have access to a mentor like Reb. Volleyball coaches who want to learn to better prepare their athletes for the demands of volleyball, but don't have the time to filter through the overwhelming amount of strength and conditioning information available online.

This book is also for the strength and conditioning professional looking to sharpen their knowledge of training for the sport. It's for the parent wanting what's best for their son or daughter. It's for the high performing volleyball player seeking a resource that can differentiate them from the competition.

But mostly, this book is for the volleyball player devastated after not making a team who refuses to give up.

CHAPTER ONE:
WHAT IS STRENGTH AND CONDITIONING FOR A VOLLEYBALL ATHLETE?

In a world full of misinformation on the topic, let's open the discussion with six things that strength and conditioning for a volleyball athlete *is not*. Allow me to preface this by saying that many of the statements that follow challenge "conventional wisdom," *aka the way we've always done it.* Several of these views I once held and acted upon myself, so understand that the information that follows is not an indictment of you or your coaching methods. Rather, it is a call to learn where traditional training methodologies miss the mark and how they can be improved.

Without further delay...

#1: STRENGTH AND CONDITIONING FOR VOLLEYBALL ATHLETES IS NOT "SPORT-SPECIFIC TRAINING."

Whoever sold the idea of sport specificity is likely great at marketing while simultaneously having a poor understanding of long-term athletic development (LTAD). Often, this idea of sport specificity errantly manifests itself as an attempt to perform a sport skill with load or resistance. These endeavors, while well-intentioned, quite often miss the mark when it comes to creating favorable adaptations that will increase a volleyball player's chances of success in their sport.

The idea of sport specificity originates from Yuri Verkhoshansky and Mel Siff's term *dynamic correspondence.* This concept, presented in their book *Supertraining,* refers to a movement's or a training program's ability to confer positive physiological adaptations that will translate to improved sport performance.

To put that in more relatable terms: despite my earlier statement against misguided attempts at sport specificity, make no mistake–the training program must consider and address the key performance indicators (KPIs) in the sport of volleyball. Our efforts should translate to improvements on the court, otherwise they are a waste of time.

According to Verkhoshansky and Siff, the degree to which this transfer will occur depends on 5 factors:

1. The amplitude and direction of movement.
    a. What joint actions and ranges of motion are required during the movement?
    b. In what planes of motion does the movement occur?

2. The accentuated region of force production.
    a. Where within the movement is force produced? What about peak force?

3. The dynamics of effort of the movement.
    a. Does the effort match what is required by the sporting movement?

4. The rate and time of maximal force production.
    a. Is the rate of force development (RFD) the same as what is required by the sporting movement?

5. The regime of muscular work.
    a. What type of contractions are involved and when?
    b. Is the stretch-shortening cycle used?
    c. What energy systems are used?
    d. Is the movement cyclical or acylical?

Don't understand a word of this? Worry not–despite claiming it as our industry's Bible, most of those in the strength and conditioning community never finished *Supertraining* anyway, so you're not alone. Which brings me to my point:

The concept of sport specificity in training came from ideas that most don't understand. It has since been extrapolated into what I would define as "sport mimicry" and quite simply has very little transfer of training to sport, or to use our newly-learned term, *dynamic correspondence.*

Here's an example:

I once worked with a program that used contraptions they called "the leaper." This was a custom-designed, velcro training belt that featured padded neoprene ankle and wrist cuffs. The cuffs were attached to the waist belt with approximately 18-inches of hot pink resistance tubing, and really...who doesn't love hot pink? Volleyball athletes were to wear these fashion-forward devices for plyometric training sessions during which they would complete spike approaches, quite often under tremendous fatigue.

The problem?

As a starting point, the resistance on the tubing was heavy enough that very few athletes could complete an arm swing with anything even moderately resembling a full range of motion. The few athletes that could muscle through the resistance did so with an abysmally slow arm swing. What appeared to be sport specific to the untrained eye was an atrocity to anyone with a basic knowledge of the principle of dynamic correspondence.

In addition to the fact that most things labeled as "sport specific" are far from it, I would venture to guess that many reading this book work with athletes of a low training age. For those unfamiliar, an athlete's training age is the number of years they have consistently participated in a strength and conditioning program geared towards LTAD. It is not the same as biological age, nor is it the same as the number of years they have played sports. It is important to understand that what is appropriate for elite level athletes with an advanced training age is not always appropriate for younger, lesser-trained athletes.

In fact, at lower training ages/stages of development, much simpler training programs focusing on basic movement competencies will elicit tremendous training adaptations. Phrased another way: lower level athletes don't need more specialized training methods to see improvements. *They don't need "sport specificity."* Instead, they need a training program that emphasizes general athletic development.

But don't take it from me–people much smarter have created graphics to illustrate these concepts.

Figure 1 shows Dr. Anatoliy Bondarchuk's exercise classification system in pyramid form. In this pyramid, general movements and exercises serve as the foundation for more specific exercises that are applicable later in an athlete's career, when those more specific means are actually needed to elicit training adaptations.

To evaluate this pyramid further, only the two lower tiers of the pyramid (GPE and SPE) are strength and conditioning related activities. The next two tiers are elements that closely resemble parts of the actual game, and the final tier is the game itself. I will say that the lines get blurred between S&C and sport skill in the special development exercise (SDE) tier, but exercises like these are well outside of the scope of this book, as they are outside of the scope of what developmental athletes need. In truth, in my experience, these SDE exercises were outside of the scope of what most Division I volleyball players need as well. Basics work, and they work for a really long time.

COMPETITIVE EXERCISE
Exercises that are identical or nearly identical to a game. Examples: controlled scrimmages or drills that train the cognitive-perceptual elements of the game.

SPECIFIC DEVELOPMENT EXERCISE
Exercises that mirror the game, but broken into its component elements. These exercises may or may not include specific strength exercises. Examples: drills focusing on fundamental skills like passing or attacking or setting a weighted volleyball.

SPECIFIC PREPARATORY EXERCISE
Exercises that don't resemble the game, but train the major muscle groups and physiological systems involved. Examples: jumps/plyometrics, sprints, medicine ball throws, and change of direction work.

GENERAL PREPARATORY EXERCISE
Exercises that don't imitate the game or its specific systems. These all-purpose exercises train basic biomotor capacities.
Examples: strength training, mobility work, and conditioning.

EVENT

Competitive Exercise (CE)

Specific Development Exercise (SDE)

Specific Preparatory Exercise (SPE)

General Preparatory Exercise (GPE)

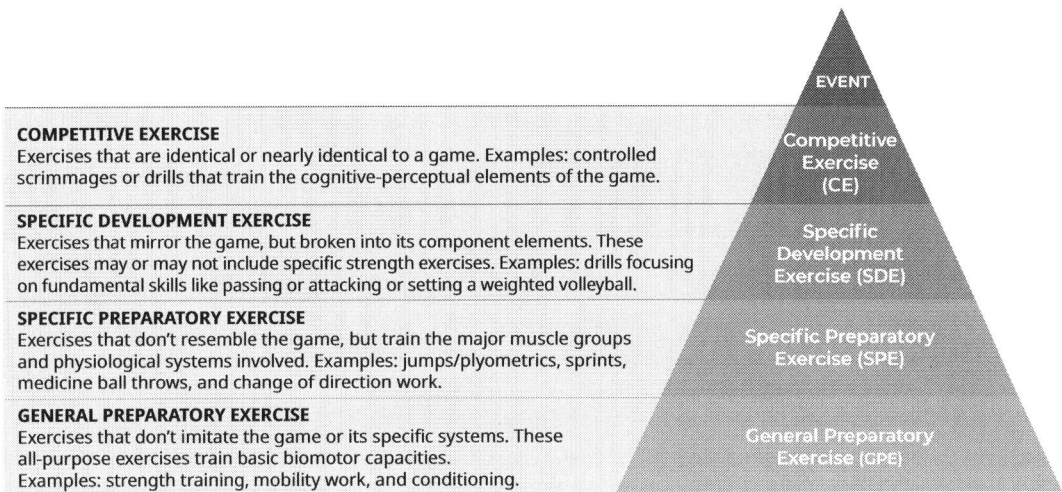

Adapted from Anatoliy Bondarchuk's Exercise Classification system as seen at https://complementarytraining.net/strength-training-categorization-part-2/

Figure 1: Anatoliy Bondarchuk's Exercise Classification system

Circling back to training age, Figures 2 & 3 provide frameworks for the relative emphasis of various physical capacities at different stages of development. It's important to note that no two-dimensional model can perfectly account for the individual differences seen in athletes due to either different rates of maturation or different training histories. However, generally speaking, athletes from adolescence to early adulthood should place a heavy emphasis in the training process on the basic physical capacities of: ***agility, speed, power, strength, and hypertrophy.***

Youth Physical Development (YPD) Model For Females

Chronological Age (Years)	2	3	4	5	6	7	8	9	10	11	12	13	14	15	16	17	18	19	20	21+
Age Periods	Early Childhood			Middle Childhood					Adolescence										Adulthood	
Growth Rate	Rapid Growth ◄► Steady Growth ◄► Adolescent Spurt ◄► Decline in Growth Rate																			
Maturational Status	Years pre-PHV ◄————— PHV ————► Years post-PHV																			
Training Adaptation	Predominantly Neural (Age-Related) ◄► Combination of Neural and Hormonal (Maturity-Related)																			
Physical Qualities	FMS			FMS			FMS		FMS											
	SSS			SSS			SSS		SSS											
	Mobility			Mobility					Mobility											
	Agility			Agility					Agility							Agility				
	Speed			Speed					Speed							Speed				
	Power			Power					Power							Power				
	Strength			Strength					Strength							Strength				
	Hypertrophy								Hypertrophy		Hypertrophy						Hypertrophy			
	Endurance & MC			Endurance & MC					Endurance & MC						Endurance & MC					
Training Structure	Unstructured			Low Structure					Moderate Structure				High Structure				Very High Structure			

Adapted from The Female Youth Physical Development Model (Lloyd, Rhodri S. PhD, CSCS*D1; Oliver, Jon L. PhD2. The Youth Physical Development Model: A New Approach to Long-Term Athletic Development. Strength and Conditioning Journal 34(3):p 61-72, June 2012. | DOI: 10.1519/SSC.0b013e31825760ea)

Figure 2: The Female Youth Physical Development Model. Font size corresponds with a quality's relative importance. Light teal indicates pre-adolescent periods of development. Dark teal indicates adolescent periods of development. PHV = peak height velocity. FMS = fundamental movement skills. SSS = sport-specific skill. MC = metabolic conditioning.

Youth Physical Development (YPD) Model For Males																			
Chronological Age (Years)	2	3	4	5	6	7	8	9	10	11	12	13	14	15	16	17	18	19	20	21+
Age Periods	Early Childhood			Middle Childhood					Adolescence											Adulthood
Growth Rate	Rapid Growth ◄—► Steady Growth ◄—► Adolescent Spurt ◄—► Decline in Growth Rate																			
Maturational Status	Years pre-PHV ◄————————— PHV —————————► Years post-PHV																			
Training Adaptation	Predominantly Neural (Age-Related) ◄—► Combination of Neural and Hormonal (Maturity-Related)																			
Physical Qualities	FMS / SSS / Mobility / Agility / Speed / Power / Strength / Hypertrophy / Endurance & MC																			
Training Structure	Unstructured			Low Structure					Moderate Structure				High Structure				Very High Structure			

Figure 3: The Male Youth Physical Development Model–this is almost identical to the female youth athletic development model, differing primarily in the (on average) later onset of puberty in males.

#2: STRENGTH AND CONDITIONING FOR VOLLEYBALL IS NOT "WORKING OUT."

The flip side is that while strength and conditioning for volleyball is not "sport-specific training," it also should not mirror erratic workouts from a group fitness class. What occurs at a CrossFit box, Orangetheory facility, Camp Gladiator, or commercial gym is NOT strength and conditioning for athletes. These are workouts designed for a member of the general population that make them feel they've accomplished something, and they have! They've likely burned calories, increased some measure of fitness, and gotten tired in the process. All great things for the aging adult looking to keep active!

But does that make these types of workouts a good fit for volleyball players? Consider the following questions, the answers to which serve as my guide to all programming decisions, even after 20 years:

1. What *specific* measures of fitness will these workouts improve?

2. Are these measures of fitness key performance indicators (KPIs) for volleyball?

3. Is there a more efficient way to improve KPIs for volleyball?

Here are my answers as they relate to group fitness classes:

1. I don't know.

2. Probably not.

3. Certainly yes.

Remember: while strength and conditioning for volleyball is not sport-specific training, if what we're doing in our training program doesn't help us on the court? We've wasted valuable time.

We all have familiarity bias: a tendency to prefer what we know over what is unfamiliar, even when the unfamiliar is better. But, a coach's job is to do what's best for their athletes, even when that means stepping away from "the way we've always done it" or what worked "back when I played." Our strength and conditioning programming should reflect the best, science-based practices available to us rather than being a copy and paste from those adult group fitness classes with a primary goal of making everyone leave feeling "accomplished" (read: tired).

On that note...

#3: STRENGTH AND CONDITIONING FOR VOLLEYBALL IS NOT "THE GRIND" WITH A PRIMARY EMPHASIS ON MAKING ATHLETES TIRED.

As my friend Tony Holler often says: *Tired is the enemy, **not** the goal.* MANY of the basic motor abilities critical in the sport of volleyball, like speed, jumping ability, and upper-body power cannot be optimally developed in the presence of fatigue. More importantly, neither can sport skill.

With that being said, a strength and conditioning program must push the boundaries of an athlete's capabilities in order to produce growth. Sessions should be executed with focused intent in order to maximize favorable adaptations. This requires careful planning on the part of the coach to ensure that the environment is conducive to high levels of effort, which means allowing recovery both within the session and between training sessions.

Training environments that are hard for the sake of being hard tend to have the opposite effect, with athletes giving just enough effort to survive rather than what is required to improve relevant KPIs for their sport. Most of us have seen or directly experienced workouts like these. Post-practice "sprints" conducted at slow speeds due to fatigue. Timed 1-mile runs during the preseason to determine an athlete's conditioning level and "mental toughness." Excessive volumes of plyometrics resulting in questionable effort and sloppy landings.

There are several problems with these types of workouts. First, when subjected to this style of training, athletes are rarely able to work at a high enough output to elicit maximal gains in speed, power, and strength due to the presence of fatigue.

Let me pause here and address the elephant in the room. I understand that the above statement may induce a fair amount of cognitive dissonance if you've had success with these methods in the past. Perhaps you read it and thought: *But I've seen gains in our vertical jump and other metrics when we've done these types of workouts!*

There are two unpopular truths to keep in mind when developing training programs. First, many athletes succeed *in spite of* their training program, not *because* of it. Second, and more importantly, growth and maturation are a more potent stimulus than *any* training program. What we may actually be observing with these "gains"? Nature's magic change.

Because of the two truths above, most training programs will *appear* to cause some type of favorable adaptation in youth and developmental athletes. But are athletes benefiting as much from these programs as they could versus a different one that keeps quality and intent at the forefront? And at what cost?

Which brings me to the next issue with these types of workouts. Not only will they not produce greater gains in KPIs, they come at an enormous cost from both a metabolic and mechanical perspective.

From the metabolic standpoint, these fatigue-inducing workouts are tremendously difficult to recover from. This is particularly true in programs that implement this style of training multiple days a week. There's very little hope of today's session producing optimal gains in speed, power, and strength. There's even less hope that tomorrow's session will either. Under-recovered athletes will not benefit maximally from any training session.

From a mechanical standpoint...there are two primary concerns:

- Athletes aren't training the movement patterns required to be successful in volleyball. Jogging is *not* low-speed sprinting. It's jogging. The two activities are very different from a biomechanical standpoint. The same can be said for jumping, cutting, and landing. To think that athletes are going to become better at these skills by completing them with altered mechanics due to fatigue makes no sense whatsoever. It's the equivalent of letting a volleyball drill devolve to the point that the entire back row is standing straight up trying to dig the ball and believing this will somehow improve defensive skill.
- Perhaps more concerning is the amount of needless stress these types of workouts place on a volleyball player's body. To reiterate, I'm not against hard work. Putting stress on an athlete's body is a necessary part of training. But there needs to be a *clear* purpose to this stress. As an example, if

I'm prescribing plyometrics or jumps in a volleyball player's training program, it will be with the goal of either:

- Teaching them how to dissipate forces effectively when landing.
- Improving maximal jump height.
- Improving reactive strength.

I can accomplish *zero* of those training goals effectively while athletes are in a state of fatigue. By attempting to, I'm placing mechanical stress on a volleyball player's already over-stressed tissues for *nothing*. I'm risking stress fractures of the lower leg and low back, tendonitis, ACL tears, and more...for *nothing*.

Negligence at its finest.

Circling back to the first bullet point, the senseless mechanical stress these workouts place on the athlete's body is exacerbated by the altered movement mechanics that occur due to fatigue. Rather than use the intended musculature to produce and dissipate force? With poor movement patterns, players will default to using less efficient systems (incorrect muscles, ligaments, etc.) in order to get the job done. A recipe for overuse injuries.

To bring that all home, it's not just that these "hard for the sake of being hard" environments produce subpar gains in speed, power, and strength...it's that they are *actively* sabotaging one's ability to improve these qualities.

#4: STRENGTH AND CONDITIONING FOR VOLLEYBALL IS NOT JUST ABOUT *TODAY*.

I get it. We all want our 11U volleyball players ready to bounce the gold-medal winning kill on the 10-foot line at the Olympics RIGHT NOW–but, doing too much too soon is a recipe for injury. Very simply, injuries occur because of an inability of the athlete's tissues to tolerate the stress they are repeatedly exposed to. Their body cannot yet handle the volume and/or intensity that it is being subjected to, because it has not been trained to do so.

Progressively increasing the body's tolerance to stress is not a process that can be rushed. Said another way: *full-time consistency beats part-time intensity.*

I often see a rushed training process in programs that relegate strength and conditioning to the off-season, ignoring the weight room during the competitive season either due to a "lack of time" or a fear of soreness.

I'll first address the "lack of time" crisis with a favorite saying from my husband: *we find time for the things that are important to us.* An in-season strength and conditioning program is absolutely important for volleyball athletes and should be a priority. Why? As Zach Dechant, author of *Movement Over Maxes,* frequently states: *the competitive season is the longest uninterrupted block of training available.* By not training during the season, a tremendous opportunity to continue developing volleyball players into better athletes is missed. What an absolute shame!

It's an even bigger shame to lose the hard-earned gains made during the off-season simply because a small amount of time wasn't allocated to strength and conditioning during the season. In fact, ignoring S&C during the season often results in players and teams being at their *absolute worst* athletically when the season demands that they are at their *absolute best.*

Don't believe me? Take a moment to consider residual training effects, or how long a given physiological adaptation lasts once you've stopped training it.

Residual Training Effects

Motor Ability	Retention	Physiological
Oxidative Energy System	30±5	Increased number of aerobic enzymes, mitochondria, capillary density, hemoglobin capacity, glycogen storage, higher rate of fat metabolism.
Strength	30±5	Improvement of neural mechanism, muscle hypertrophy
Glycolytic Energy System	18±4	Increased anaerobic enzymes, buffering capacity and glycogen storage, higher possibility of lactate accumulation
Repeat-Power	15±5	Improved aerobic/anaerobic enzymes, improved local blood circulation and lactate tolerance, repeat sprint ability
ATP/CR-P	5±3	Enhanced resynthesis of CR-P
Speed	5±3	Improved neuromuscular interactions and motor control, increases anaerobic power

Adapted from: Issurin, V. (2008). "Block Periodization: Breakthrough in Sports Training." New York, NY: Ultimate Athlete Concepts.

Figure 4: Residual training effects. The retention number in the table above is the number of days until a capacity begins to regress if it's not actively being addressed through training.

While it's all important, from a volleyball perspective, the final three rows of that table are the most concerning. In as little as *two days* of not addressing speed in training, it will decrease. As will the ability to resynthesize ATP, your muscles' energy source. ATP resynthesis allows athletes to repeat speed, power, and strength outputs, a critical ability in the sport of volleyball. Because of the decline in function of the ATP-PCr system–along with a decline in function of the other energy systems–in as few as ten days, the ability to repeat high power outputs deteriorates.

To summarize: the moment you stop strength and conditioning sessions, the countdown to having lesser-prepared athletes begins.

Imagine finishing the season losing a match you shouldn't have lost, to an opponent you beat earlier in the season. Or, losing 15-13 in set 5 to opponents of relatively equal skill, a team that you could have beaten.

Maybe you've felt this pain as an athlete or a coach. Maybe it made you vow for a better tomorrow. Maybe that tomorrow included crushing athletes in the initial stages of the off-season because "we have to get better!!" Maybe this led to injury, burnout, or the perception that S&C does little more than induce an enormous amount of fatigue and soreness. Attempting to rush the training process is a vicious cycle, but one that can easily be broken.

How? By simply *training year-round*. Realistically, you have about 6-weeks from the time your season ends until your athletes start their next competitive season. What if we didn't try to cram 52 weeks of gains into that 6-week off-season? What if we spread that over the 52 weeks available to us? It makes too much sense.

In addition to a perceived lack of time, the second concern with training during the competitive season I commonly hear in the volleyball community is the fear of soreness. This, in my opinion, has its roots in the above-mentioned training cycle, where strength and conditioning is feast or famine, versus a year-round process.

Athletes won't get sore from the weight room during the season if:

- *They train year-round in a well-designed strength and conditioning system.* A well-designed system is, among other things, one that doesn't change simply for the sake of change (read: the coaching staff gets bored so they mix it up).
- *The athlete's overall volume of training is considered and managed.* This includes practice, games, and strength and conditioning.

In truth, rarely (if ever) is it the 20-30 minute weight room session that makes athletes sore in-season. Instead, this soreness originates from a mismanaged training process.

Allow me to clarify. By "mismanaged training process," I mean 2.5-3 hour practices being the rule rather than the exception. This tradition of overly long practices needs to end. At some point, the fatigue these practices induce day after day is more than an athlete can recover from, and soreness sets in. All too often in these scenarios, rather than address the actual culprits–inefficient practice plans and poor overall load management–the weight room becomes the scapegoat and gets eliminated.

But worry not–there's a quick fix that will eliminate both the issues of fatigue/soreness and time constraints!

Simply reduce practice volume by 20-30 minutes twice a week and implement an in-season strength and conditioning program in its place.

"But, but, but…Missy, we need that practice time!"

No, you don't. I either directly trained or wrote training programs for three Texas high school state championship programs between 2019 and 2022. All three trained during their competitive season. Some might rebut with *"well, they have better players so they can afford to give up practice time for S&C!"* I'll counter by saying that, *because* they have better players, you can't afford *not* to continue building better athletes during the season through S&C. You're going to have to find that one extra edge if you want to beat opponents of equal or greater skill. Period.

Another common pattern of rushing the training process takes place when coaches attempt to use more advanced training methods on athletes with low training ages. By doing this, athletes are robbed of needed exposure to the simpler, training-age appropriate progressions that build a strong foundation for these more advanced training methods, if and when they ever are needed.

Here's an example: depth jumps are a type of plyometric where the athlete steps off of a box that measures greater than the height of their vertical jump. Upon landing, the athlete immediately jumps as high as they can. This method typically produces significant gains in both the athlete's vertical jump and reactive strength (the latter being an important capacity, as it relates to the ability to jump multiple times in series, as well as rapidly change directions).

If we *only* look at the rewards of using this method, we might believe this is an appropriate inclusion in the training program of lesser developed athletes. After all, we want to drive athlete motivation (and validate our own programming) by demonstrating results!

But only looking at a training method's rewards without assessing its risks is poor practice.

Depth jumps place an enormous amount of stress on an athlete's joints and soft tissues. If they haven't trained in a way that prepares them to withstand this stress? They are at a greater risk for injury. Athletes of low training age, by definition, have not been prepared to handle this stress.

Further, they will more than likely default to the use of suboptimal mechanics when completing these jumps, because they were never taught the correct way to jump and land in the first place. There is often an assumption that athletes will just "figure out" the basics as they go along–and they usually do, but with compensatory movement patterns that will stunt their progress down the road. Jumping is an *ability* and a *skill*, and skills must be taught and practiced.

And by the way...trading long-term progress for short-term results is the outcome for the *lucky* ones. For the *unlucky* ones, this unstable foundation of poor movement patterns results in either an overuse or catastrophic injury, maybe even both. What a tragedy.

The even more tragic thing for athletes subjected to advanced training means before they're ready? It was *completely* unnecessary. It will likely be many years (if ever) before an athlete needs exposure to advanced training methods. While I can't give an exact timeline for every athlete, I can tell you that in seven years at the Division I level, I never saw the well run dry on progress in basic training methods with volleyball players. The methods and underlying principles in this book will work for a really long time.

With that in mind, here's my recommendation:

Think carefully before attempting to apply advanced training strategies to undeveloped trainees. Then, after careful consideration, don't do it.

Always have an athlete's long-term athletic development in mind. This means that just because an athlete *can* do something, that doesn't mean they *should*. Also, just because basic training methods seem mundane (or bore you as a coach), that doesn't mean it's time to move on. Remember: half of the team won't remember the warm-up after doing it every single day for six months. Every day is a brand new day with adolescent athletes. Train accordingly.

#5: STRENGTH AND CONDITIONING FOR VOLLEYBALL IS NOT A SILVER BULLET.

After spending most of this chapter hurting the feelings of sport coaches, it's very important that I don't exempt strength and conditioning professionals from finding themselves in my crosshairs.

Strength and conditioning coaches LOVE to talk about "injury prevention." I did too. First 10 years of my coaching career? Zero ACL tears among the athletes I trained. Not one. My ego could hardly fit through the door. My program was above reproach and I took the floor on game nights with an air of superiority each and every time an opponent had an athlete wearing a knee brace. *"Not on my watch,"* I would think to myself, and *"not on my program."* The burden of already knowing everything at just 32-years-old was heavy, but I carried it with confidence and style.

And then one night my husband found me at our dining table at 2:00 a.m., teardrops soaking into the paper towel I'd used as a coaster for my drink. It had happened. "Something is wrong with my program," I sputtered. "It failed. Jada tore her ACL tonight. I failed her. Tomorrow I have to look at all of my programs and find out why."

In truth, something is wrong with every program, but that's not what caused this injury. The athlete in question had a previous ACL tear. In her immediate family there had been a total of eight ACL reconstruction surgeries. The surgeon stated that her femoral notch was such that this was not a scenario of *if* she tore her ACL, but *when* would it happen. The "failure" of my training program didn't cause this injury. If anything, it might have delayed the inevitable.

Genetics matter. Training history matters. Catastrophic injuries happen. While a well-designed strength and conditioning program will reduce the likelihood of an athlete becoming injured, it simply cannot prevent all injuries, nor can it "cure" them. A fraying rotator cuff will still be a fraying rotator cuff (and soon be a torn RC) if the faulty movement patterns and overuse of the athlete's shoulder are not addressed.

In addition to not having magical healing powers, a strength and conditioning program cannot turn water into wine. One of the most important determinants of success in volleyball, particularly in the front row? Height. Strength and conditioning can't teach tall. It can, however, better equip a player to compete at a smaller size by improving their vertical jump and reactive strength.

A second determinant of success? Sport-specific skill. Strength and conditioning may not be teaching serve receive, but it can add to the effective radius a passer can cover, thereby increasing their serve receive percentage. Marginal improvements like this one could determine which side of 15-13 your team finds itself on in the 5th set.

#6: STRENGTH AND CONDITIONING FOR VOLLEYBALL IS NOT ROCKET SCIENCE.

The strength and conditioning industry has done a tremendous job of gatekeeping our craft. We have stacks of Russian training manuals on our shelves, sprint kinogram pillow cases, and most importantly we take the simplest principles through a rebrand every few years so we can praise ourselves for "new" methods. We believe we are the only life form intelligent enough to design and implement training programs.

We're wrong on that last part...mostly.

In truth, strength coaches are absolutely better equipped to do this than 99% of sport coaches (for my track and field coaches reading: yes, you too) simply because we have devoted our lives to the study of this field and remain current in our practices. Sport coaches, on the other hand, are devoting their lives to the study of their sport.

This is as it should be and it is unlikely that either party will ever demonstrate the same mastery of the other party's craft.

However...if a volleyball coach can teach a setter to take a pass that's spinning 15 feet in the air, and stop it with their fingertips all the while actively decelerating their body to get their feet into position, then redirect that ball into a 6-inch by 6-inch area in space determined by both the hitter's preferences and the opposing team's block...you'll never convince me that same coach can't learn enough to safely lead that athlete through a strength and conditioning program if provided the knowledge and tools to do so.

They 100% can and this book will show you how.

SO WHAT EXACTLY IS STRENGTH AND CONDITIONING FOR VOLLEYBALL?

From our analysis of what strength and conditioning for volleyball is *not*, we should be able to draw some conclusions about what it is!

✗ Volleyball S&C *IS NOT*...sport-specific training
✓ Volleyball S&C *IS*...**general athletic development**

This raises a player's ceiling for the acquisition and improvement of sport skill!

✗ Volleyball S&C *IS NOT*...random workouts or those with ill-defined goals
✓ Volleyball S&C *IS*...**a progressive system targeting specific physiological adaptations**

This guarantees the athlete's precious time and energy are spent on things that matter most and sessions are conducted with an emphasis on technical proficiency and high levels of focus and intent.

✗ Volleyball S&C *IS NOT*...a short-term process
✓ Volleyball S&C *IS*...**a year-round process that allows athletes to accumulate quality training that will leave them prepared in the long term**

This allows you to slow-cook the training process. To use a baking analogy: if I'm baking a cake, I can't turn the oven up twice as hot and cook it twice as fast. Doing this will lead to burning the cake, damage that cannot be undone.

✗ Volleyball S&C *IS NOT*...a cure-all
✓ Volleyball S&C *IS*...**a way to give athletes the best possible chance to stay healthy while reaching their highest potential**

The best athletic ability is availability. Consistently implemented strength and conditioning programs have been demonstrated to reduce the likelihood of an athlete becoming injured.

✗ Volleyball S&C *IS NOT*...too difficult for an already over-stretched sport coach to implement with their team
✓ Volleyball S&C *IS*...**attainable for anyone with the help of this book**

Don't let information overload through social media or gatekeeping from "gurus" discourage you from implementing a training program with your athletes. You will be hard pressed to convince me that most coaches have nothing but the best in mind for their athletes. However, when already tasked with coaching 1-2 sports, teaching 1-4 preps, managing equipment, driving a bus, and "other duties as assigned," it can be overwhelming to try to take on one more thing in order to give your athletes the best experience. But it doesn't have to be.

Volleyball coaches already know what KPIs are important for the sport:

- Lower body strength and power
- Upper body strength and power
- Core stability
- Rapid accelerations and decelerations
- The endurance to repeat the above actions across a 5 set match

The chapters that follow will show you exactly how to address them.

SECTION 1:
BASIC MOVEMENT PATTERNS AND PROGRESSIONS

Scan the QR Code to watch the Demo Videos that correspond with the Exercise Progressions and Images listed in Section 1:

CHAPTER TWO:
THE HIP HINGE

Forget what you've heard: squats have been dethroned. RDLs are the new king/queen of the weight room.

In seriousness, the hip hinge is critical in most athletic movements. Even the squat demands a proper hip hinge! From a volleyball perspective, jumping and landing require an efficient hinge in order to maximize jump height while ensuring a safe and stable landing. Passing and defensive postures are each based off of the universal athletic position (UAP), which requires the ability to separate movement at the hips from movement at the spine, aka the hip hinge. Setting the outside ball requires power from legs and hips, and as the level of play increases, jump setting becomes a more important game element to speed up the offense.

Additionally, most sports and most training programs overload the front side of the body, but the muscles of the posterior chain are critical for movement proficiency as well as injury reduction. As a result, I heavily emphasize posterior chain movements in all of the programs I write.

Hip hip hooray for hip hinges! Except...

They can really suck to teach. Handing a beginner athlete a barbell on Day One is very likely going to result in a disastrous movement pattern and a frustrated coach.

Typically in the hip hinge, this disaster manifests as significant flexion in the lumbar spine, reminiscent of an armadillo curling into a ball. As any native Texan will tell you, once an armadillo has taken up residence in your yard, they are almost impossible to get rid of without resorting to violence. The prognosis for removing hip hinge armadillos from the weight room can be equally grim. Let's avoid the arrival of this invasive species by using these five principles and starting with the beginner level progressions that follow.

HIP HINGE PRINCIPLES

1. The athlete's feet should be *hip* distance apart. Do not coach the feet "shoulder distance" apart. This is incorrect, and a hill I will die on. We want the feet placed in a "jumping stance," which is hip distance apart.

2. The knees should be slightly bent and should maintain relatively the same degree of flexion throughout the

exercise. A good rule of thumb is that at the moment that the athlete feels the need to bend their knees further (or round the spine) to achieve a greater range of motion (ROM), it is time to start the ascent of the movement.

3. The spine should be neutral. This includes the cervical spine (neck). Athletes should not be cued to "look up" during the movement–instead, their eyes should be directed straight ahead, or even at the floor 6-8 feet in front of them. The lumbar spine should be neutral and not flexed or hyperextended. Loading either of these positions potentially exposes the low back to injury risk. It can be helpful to teach lumbo-pelvic stability through anterior/posterior pelvic tilts in a supine position, a topic we will discuss in Chapter 5.

4. With feet flat, push the hips back and descend until a stretch is felt in the hamstrings.

5. Rather than focusing on scapular retraction (squeezing the shoulder blades together) which often errantly results in shrugging the shoulders, pull the bar back towards the body. This engages the lats, which assist in stabilizing the lumbar spine.

As an aside: weak/tight lats have negative implications for shoulder health, a major concern in the sport of volleyball. This will be the first place I point out that shoulder health/arm care for the volleyball athlete isn't a separate program we do with light, banded exercises–it is the result of the *entire* training program.

HIP HINGE PROGRESSION 1: THE VERTICAL PVC RDL

For this, you'll need 1" PVC pipes or dowel rods cut into 6' sections. If going the PVC route, I recommend Schedule 40 PVC, as this is thicker and more durable. A good number to have in your possession is one PVC for every 2-3 athletes.

1. Stand with the feet hip distance apart, knees slightly bent.

2. Place the PVC vertically along the spine.

3. Ensure that the PVC has 3 points of contact with the athlete's body: the back of the head, between the scapulae, and the tailbone.

4. The hands can be placed in a comfortable position*: one with an underhand grip at the low back, the other with an overhand grip either at the back of the neck or above the head. It does not matter which hand is on top and which is on bottom, but athletes will generally place their dominant/hitting arm on top due to limited shoulder internal rotation in their hitting shoulder.

5. Initiate the hip hinge by pushing the hips back and maintaining a slight bend in the knee.

6. Maintain all 3 points of contact with the PVC at all times.

7. Once a stretch is felt in the hamstrings or the athlete cannot go lower without further bending the knees or

losing the point of contact at the tailbone, begin the ascent and return to the starting position.

8. Repeat for 8-10 reps.

The PVC provides the athlete with an external cue that offers immediate feedback as to whether or not they have completed the exercise properly. External cueing is an extremely effective strategy with beginner athletes. Often, internal cues like "back flat/chest out" are less effective because the athletes have no pre-existing mental model of these movements and, more importantly, very little awareness of where their bodies are in space. Further, having a system in place where feedback doesn't require the coach to be evaluating every single rep is incredibly valuable–when training large groups, it's impossible to simultaneously give every athlete feedback.

Common errors in this movement are:

1. A loss of contact of the PVC at one of the three points, usually the tailbone. This is occurring due to rounding/ flexing at the lumbar spine and should be fixed by simply instructing the athlete to not lose that point of contact. Let the PVC take over cueing from there.

2. Excessive knee bend. This can be fixed by cueing or by placing an object at knee height directly in front of the athlete–like a box, bench, or partner holding another PVC–and instructing the athlete to not allow their knees to touch this object.

Athletes with limited shoulder mobility may need to adjust hand position slightly. Those with severely limited shoulder mobility may need to complete wall reach RDL instead (see Progression 1A).

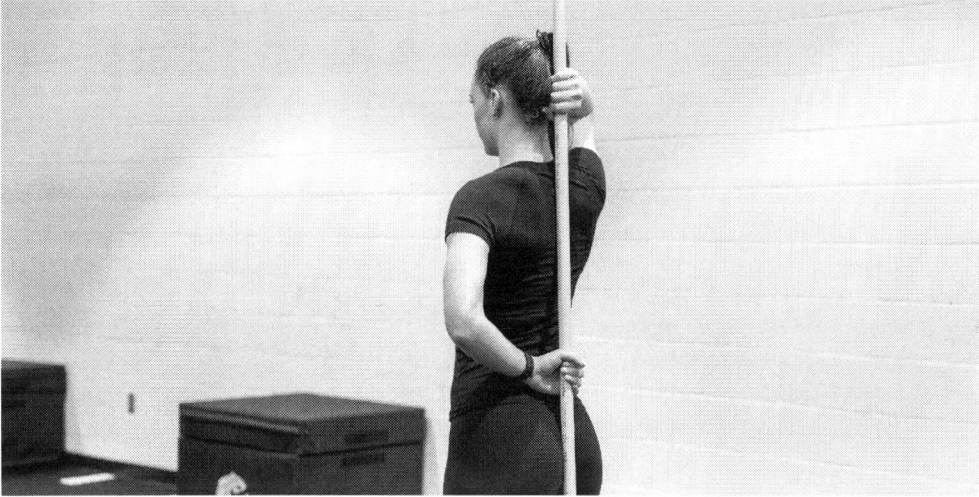

Vertical PVC RDL: 3 Points of Contact (Setup)

Vertical PVC RDL: 3 Points of Contact (Finish)

HIP HINGE PROGRESSION 1A: THE WALL REACH RDL

Though I would highly recommend the vertical PVC RDL as Step 1 in this teaching progression, certain circumstances–like limited shoulder ROM or limited equipment–may necessitate an alternate approach.

Enter the wall-reach RDL.

1. Stand, facing away, about 6" from a wall or other object at hip height. You may have to alter this distance slightly to accommodate the wide range of heights among athletes in a volleyball program.

2. Place the feet hip distance apart with the knees slightly bent.

3. Reach back and touch the wall with the hips, maintaining the same degree of knee bend.

4. Once the wall is reached, return to the starting position.

5. The head should remain neutral throughout the movement.

Athletes who miss the wall are likely doing so because they are hinging from their spine versus their hips. Rather than endlessly cueing them to "push their hips back," likely to no avail, we are using the wall as an external cue to provide feedback.

Wall Reach RDL (Setup)

Wall Reach RDL (Finish)

HIP HINGE PROGRESSION 2: THE HORIZONTAL PVC RDL

This is a somewhat controversial step, as many think it isn't necessary. Not only do I think it's necessary, but I also tend to operate under the assumption that it is better to have something and not need it than to need it and not have it.

The reason I include this step is that after a tremendous amount of trial and error, I've determined that the best practice with beginner-level trainees is to manipulate only *one* variable at a time. This classic behavioral shaping principle is one I ignored for years, believing that moving straight from the vertical PVC to the barbell was changing only one variable. It's not. Doing this is manipulating two variables: the placement of the implement and the weight of the implement. Additionally, the horizontal PVC RDL allows me to teach grip width on the bar, something that has not been previously taught.

Where I may use the vertical PVC for up to 2-6 weeks, depending on the ability level of the athlete in front of me, I may only need to use the horizontal PVC for a single set before moving on to a barbell RDL.

1. Stand with the feet hip distance apart.

2. Place the hands a thumb's distance outside of the thighs, or slightly wider for those with longer arms.

3. Grip the PVC with an overhand grip on both hands.

4. Roll the knuckles down to take the slack out of the arms and pull the bar back towards the body using the lats.

5.   Slightly flex the knees and push the hips back until the athlete feels a stretch in the hamstring.

6.   Maintain a slight bend in the knees throughout the movement.

7.   The head should remain neutral and the athlete should continue to drive the PVC back toward their body to engage the lats. To clarify: the PVC should remain in contact with the legs the entire movement.

8.   Return to the starting position, contracting the glutes.

Horizontal PVC RDL (Setup)

Horizontal PVC RDL (Finish)

HIP HINGE PROGRESSION 3: THE BARBELL RDL

This will look EXACTLY like the horizontal PVC, just with a barbell in the hands. For some athletes, the transition directly to a 45 lb bar will be fine. For others, having lighter training bars available in your facility will be necessary. These can be purchased as light as 15 lbs and allow for the addition of weights to progress athletes up to a standard Olympic barbell.

BB RDL (Setup)

BB RDL (Finish)

Once you've reached this step, begin to progressively increase weight as the athlete's technique allows. An increase of 5-10 lbs weekly is usually doable. However...

At no point is it acceptable to allow technique to suffer in pursuit of more weight.

We are not training powerlifters or weightlifters. (Even then, I would heavily discourage the allowance of technical breakdown.) We are focusing on improving sport performance. This cannot occur if an athlete is sidelined due to injury.

With that constraint in place, remember that hip hinges are incredibly important in sport movements. RDLs in particular train eccentric hamstring strength, an important consideration for inoculating the hamstring against injury and also to protect the knee from injury. Because of this, I consider the RDL a primary movement that needs to be loaded relatively heavy once an athlete has progressed to that point.

HIP HINGE PROGRESSION 4: THE STAGGERED STANCE RDL

The single-leg RDL is a highly technical exercise that has all of the requirements of the RDL plus a need for balance, stability of the ankle and knee, and the ability to control hip internal and external rotation throughout the movement. While a great exercise, it is extremely challenging to teach and load with beginner-level athletes. Full disclosure: it is extremely challenging to teach and load with Division I athletes as well. A great workaround is to use the staggered stance RDL, which allows you to load a single-leg hip hinge without the interference of balance.

1. Stand with the feet hip distance apart.

2. Hold either a barbell or 2 dumbbells.

3. Stagger one foot back so that the toe of the back foot lines up with the arch of the front foot, maintaining a hip-width stance.

4. Perform an RDL with the weight in the front foot. The back foot serves as a "kickstand" and no effort needs to be made to keep it flat on the floor.

5. Keep the hips and shoulders squared forward over both legs.

Staggered DB RDL (Setup)

Staggered DB RDL (Finish)

HIP HINGE PROGRESSION 5: TRUE SINGLE-LEG RDL VARIANTS

5A: PVC Single-Leg RDL

If I am going to progress an athlete into single-leg RDL's, I begin again by using a step that includes the external cue of a PVC.

Instructions for completion of the PVC single-leg RDL are as follows:

1. Begin standing on two legs with a PVC placed on the toe of the non-working leg. This toe should be pulled toward the shin, or dorsiflexed.

Slight tangent: the working leg is the one *staying on the ground* while completing the exercise. The non-working leg is the one acting as a pendulum during the movement. The one that is *moving*. You will have to explain this AT LENGTH to athletes if you choose to use this exercise. Something to keep in mind if you aren't in possession of a lot of patience or you lack the funding to get your prematurely graying hair colored on a regular basis.

2. The PVC should be held in the same-side hand of the non-working leg. (If it's on your right toe, it should be in your right hand). The hand holding the PVC should be approximately rib-cage height.

3. Engage the lat, just as you have done previously in a barbell RDL.

4. Contract the glute of the non-working leg and keep this leg relatively straight throughout the movement.

5. Slightly bend the knee of the working leg.

6. Begin to hinge forward, keeping shoulders and hips level.

PVC Single Leg RDL (Setup)

PVC Single Leg RDL (Finish)

An extremely common error is to rotate the body towards the non-working leg. This may be fixed by cueing the athlete to keep the back toe pointed straight towards the ground throughout the movement, or it may be an inability of the athlete to achieve and/or maintain sufficient hip internal rotation. If the latter is the case, the staggered single-leg RDL variant may be better suited for the athlete at this time.

5B: Dumbbell Single-Leg RDL

Having learned the movement pattern of the single-leg RDL, we can begin incorporating load.

1. Hold one dumbbell or kettlebell in the hand opposite the working leg OR hold two implements, one in each hand.

2. Engage the lat and "shorten" the arm against the load.

3. Hinge at the hip.

4. Keep the hips and shoulders squared forward, so that the back toe stays pointed straight at the ground.

5. DO NOT allow the dumbbell or kettlebell to touch the ground. Let me model repeating this for you, because you will have to say it no less than 80,000 times a day if you choose to include this in your program: *do not allow the DB or KB to touch the ground.* This represents one of the following technical flaws: a loss of tension in the lat, hinging at the spine instead of the hip, or excessive knee bend.

Single Leg DB RDL (Setup)

Single Leg DB RDL (Finish)

A WORD ON TRAP BAR DEADLIFTS

This is a decision you're going to need to make in your own program.

These days, most weight rooms have a fairly large number of trap bars and many coaches praise the trap bar deadlift (TBDL) for how easy it is to teach. The lift is also praised as a great method to teach athletes how to apply force into the ground. For these reasons, the use of the TBDL is widespread. For many, it's the first hip hinge they teach athletes. For me it's the last.

I'm going to list my reasons for teaching it later in the training process, then discuss where I've finally landed on its use.

1. Because athletes can generally move a lot of weight in this exercise, they try to move a lot of weight long before they are ready to. I'm not in the business of ego lifting, I'm in the business of putting championship programs on the floor. My athletes can have all the ego that they want bouncing balls at the net and stealing the souls of their opponents with digs in the backfield, but we have to be healthy to do it.

    Ego makes idiots of us all in the weight room, so I nip that in the bud with exercise selection (RDLs instead of TBDL), particularly in the early phases of training.

2. Unlike most lifts, the TBDL starts with the concentric portion of the lift. There is no "preload" through the

eccentric phase. If athletes do not start the lift braced and with proper intent? They will gain mechanical advantage any way they can, usually by flexing at the lumbar spine. As previously stated, this is a recipe for injury. While the necessity to set up properly is far from unique in the TBDL, I find it to be much more critical in this lift. If I unrack a heavy squat? I feel the load immediately and figure out real quick I better get tight before starting the rep. That feedback is missing when initiating the TBDL.

3. Over the years, I've had more parental complaints about the TBDL than any other exercise. The reason is simple: they hear the word *deadlift* and hit the panic button. They were *once* told that deadlifts are bad for your back, and in the absence of evidence to the contrary, internalized this fear-mongering as a universal truth.

   This book is not about platitudes–this book is about strength and conditioning in the real world. While I'm not going to allow the peanut gallery to dictate my programming, I am going to take a hard look at which battles I want to fight as a coach because there will be *many*. No, the TBDL isn't an inherently bad exercise. Yes, it can be flawlessly coached and flawlessly executed. Yes, parents and athletes alike can be provided with education. But it can be challenging, and in some cases nearly impossible to battle through long-held biases, particularly when the torches and pitchforks ("2-weeks no weight room full-go on court" chiropractor's notes) are already in hand and the mob is approaching.

All that being said, despite a large portion of the S&C community acting like the TBDL is the second coming of Christ, I *only* implement it later in the training program of my volleyball players once I have a fairly wide base of strength built and, more importantly, athlete buy-in.

The "C" in S&C shouldn't be for controversy. Or chiropractor's notes.

CHAPTER THREE:
THE SQUAT

Speaking of controversy...let's talk about the squat!

But, first we need to park our time machine and leave the keys back in 1961 when the study that produced the "deep squats are bad for your knees" nonsense originated.

Since then, a much different story has emerged.

Degrees of Knee Flexion During the Deep Squat

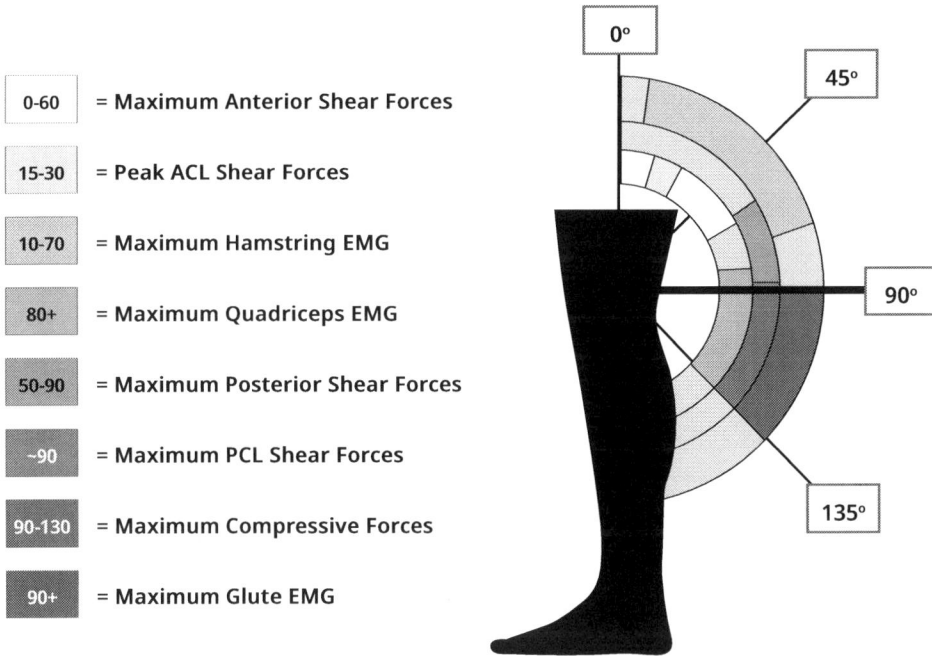

0-60	= Maximum Anterior Shear Forces
15-30	= Peak ACL Shear Forces
10-70	= Maximum Hamstring EMG
80+	= Maximum Quadriceps EMG
50-90	= Maximum Posterior Shear Forces
~90	= Maximum PCL Shear Forces
90-130	= Maximum Compressive Forces
90+	= Maximum Glute EMG

Figure 5: Forces on the knee at various joint angles. Adapted from Physical Therapist Aaron Swanson's consolidation of multiple published research studies.

The graphic above adapted from physical therapist Aaron Swanson shows the results from a number of published studies that looked at various joint angles and the forces encountered at the knee in each one.

A key takeaway on this, from a study published by Escamilla in 2012, is that ACL stress and anterior shear are highest when performing partial ROM squats, between 10 and 30 degrees of knee flexion. ACL stress is not exactly what we're looking to achieve with our squat, nor is limited quad and glute activation, which as shown above doesn't peak until the knee is past 80 degrees of flexion. (I will note that the tension in the ACL in a half squat is well below the threshold limit to cause a rupture, so please do not mistake this information as fear mongering.

Partial ROM squats are actually used out of necessity in the return to play process of ACL reconstruction patients. Rather, this is a statement against the "deep squats are bad for your knees" mindset.)

There is one tradeoff...full ROM squats are where the knee encounters the greatest compressive forces at the patellofemoral joint. However, a 2019 study by Wu et al., showed that the hamstring-on-calf position in a full range of motion squat (aka "ass to grass") helps reduce forces at the patellofemoral and tibiofemoral joints by 42% and 57% respectively.

So what does all of this mean? It means the answer to squat depth is: "it depends." If an athlete has the range of motion to get into a full range of motion squat, there absolutely are benefits to strengthening the body at end range. If unable to achieve a full ROM, we will work towards that–but never to the detriment of safety and proper technique. In reality, volleyball frequently puts an athlete's hip, knee, and ankle joints in extreme ranges of motion. To not have strength in these ranges and be forced into them during the course of play can be a recipe for injury. This is another case where I feel that it is better to have something and not need it–in this case a full ROM squat–than to need it and not have it.

Further, when selecting our squat strategy, coaches must understand that athletes tend to be very quad/knee dominant. With the hamstring playing a critical role in the protection of the ACL, we need to cue athletes to move at the hip first and sit back while squatting. Not only does this motion strengthen the hamstrings to a greater degree, it also reduces patellofemoral compression and ACL strain during the squat.

Caution must be used, however, because there is once again a tradeoff. When sitting the hips back, the torso must lean forward as a counterbalance. By going too far in this direction, a great amount of stress is placed on the lumbar spine. This is of particular concern to me with volleyball athletes for a couple of reasons:

1. A primary volleyball KPI? Height, which often comes with relatively long femurs. The result? In order to achieve depth in the squat, taller athletes will need to sit back even further, creating more forward lean through the torso and greater stress on the lumbar spine.

2. Whether it is typical to classify it this way or not, volleyball is a rotational sport. While protecting the lumbar spine is a concern for me with all athletes, it is of particularly great concern with rotational athletes who encounter tremendous loads on their spines already. We will revisit the concept of spine health in Chapter 11.

A lumbar spine injury can end a volleyball player's career prematurely. Even worse? It can subject that athlete to a lifetime of pain.

But here's the good news: there's a solution that checks all of the previously addressed boxes:

Stop back squatting and adopt front squatting instead.

Front squats have been found to reduce stress in the lumbar spine as well as the knee joints compared to back squats, without compromising strength development in the quads and glutes. Sure, there's slightly less hamstring activation, but we're going to train the hamstrings enough through hip hinge variants and sprinting.

Additionally, the front squat puts the bar in a more shoulder-friendly position for many athletes than the back squat. This is yet another way we can address shoulder health in volleyball players through our overall training program, and not just a few specific exercises.

Regardless of the specific type of squat used, the following principles hold true:

BASIC PRINCIPLES OF THE SQUAT

1. Stance width in general will be slightly wider than shoulder width. Some athletes will prefer either a narrower or wider stance, but generally speaking, this is a good starting point for most.

2. The feet should be neutral or rotated out slightly, about 0-10 degrees.

3. The whole foot should remain in contact with the ground throughout the entire lift. In my younger years I cued "weight in your heels." However, an even weight distribution across the "tripod foot" is superior, so I now cue "feet flat."

4. The movement should be initiated by sitting back/hinging at the hip before sitting down.

5. Drive the knees out to create torque at the hip. My favorite cue for this is to "rip the floor apart with your feet." To increase understanding, I generally have athletes stand with their feet in a squat stance, bend their knees slightly, and tell them to try to rip the floor apart with their feet. Afterwards, I ask "where did you feel that?" To which most will point to their gluteus medius, an important muscle that helps stabilize the knee.

6. Keep the head neutral throughout the movement. Do not cue athletes to look up while squatting. Instead, cue them to take the wrinkles out of the back of their neck by pulling the chin back versus down.

7. Keep the core braced throughout the movement.

SQUAT PROGRESSION 1: THE COUNTERMOVEMENT SQUAT

Since I'm such a quick study, it only took 13 years for me to finally figure out the best way to teach the squat. After lackluster attempts to use a squat to a box as the first step in my teaching progression, I had the opportunity to watch a presentation by Coach Josh Hickman, a high school strength coach in the DFW area, which included his squat progression. I'd never seen a countermovement squat prior to that, but immediately determined that this was the missing link in my own teaching progression. Even if not, this method would at least free me from the annoyance of having to drag the boxes out and struggle to match each athlete to the box height that would allow them to find the proper depth (which was rarely the *proper* depth due to the limited capacity to adjust those boxes and the fact that there were never enough to go around in the first place).

Fortunately, I was accurate in my initial assessment. Implementing the countermovement squat in my teaching progression proved to be a game changer with athletes of all levels, but I found it particularly helpful at the middle school level where coaches might have over 150 athletes in a session and nowhere near enough equipment. To complete the countermovement squat, athletes could use a 5-10lb plate, a medicine ball, or even a volleyball.

For purposes of instruction, and because it's my preferred implement, the description below will assume plates are being used.

Steps are as follows:

1. Start with the feet slightly outside of shoulder distance.

2. Hold a 5 or 10 lb weight plate in both hands at the chest.

3. Initiate the movement by hinging at the hip, sitting back.

4. At the same pace that the hips are moving back and down, press the plate out in front of the body so that the arms are fully extended at the bottom of the squat.

5. CUE: "Push your hips away from the plate."

6. Finish with the arms parallel to the floor.

7. Keep the feet flat and head neutral throughout the entire movement.

8. Descend until maximum depth is attained, spreading the floor with the feet.

9. Return to start, bringing the plate back to the chest as the hips rise.

Countermovement Squat (Setup)

Countermovement Squat (Finish)

What I love about this movement? Many things. First, beginner athletes often struggle to master the concept of pushing the hips back. They feel they will fall over backwards, as this pattern is foreign to many knee-dominant athletes. Extending the plate away from the body eliminates this fear before it ever begins. Additionally, cueing the hips away from the plate is another external cue, and one that I've found far more effective than the internal cue of "sit the hips back." Finally, even adding a small load in the hands forces the athlete to brace the core during the movement, a critical element of protecting the lumbar spine.

SQUAT PROGRESSION 2: THE GOBLET SQUAT

The next step in the squat progression is the goblet squat. Here, we can begin to incorporate more load. Typically, depending on the athlete, they will start holding somewhere between 10 and 40 pounds. I recognize that this is quite the range, but your program will very likely have *quite the range* of athletes, and I can't tell you what will work for each.

Operate from a place of common sense: the smaller and weaker the athlete, the lighter the starting weight. Likewise, the lower the training age, the lighter the starting weight. In general, err on the side of too light and adjust from there. This process is like seasoning your food–you can easily add more salt, but removing it requires more of an effort. Once an athlete has held a heavier weight in their hands and believes they can lift it, convincing their ego that they shouldn't because their form is awful becomes a challenge. "I got this coach!" is all too often the mantra of athletes who do not, in fact, have this.

Steps to the goblet squat are as follows:

1. Hold a kettlebell (by the horns) or a dumbbell (by the head) with the hands in front of the chest.

2. Complete the squat pattern as described above.

3. Progress in weight ~2.5-5 lbs per week as the athlete's technique allows.

Goblet Squat (Setup)

Goblet Squat (Finish)

SQUAT PROGRESSION 3: THE HANDS-FREE BARBELL FRONT SQUAT, AKA "ZOMBIE" SQUAT

One of the most difficult concepts for an athlete to master when beginning to front squat is learning the front rack position. In my opinion, this has a twofold point of origin:

1. The sheer unfamiliarity of this position, which leads them down the path of discomfort.

2. The fear that if they aren't death gripping the bar, they're going to drop it.

Using the hands-free barbell front squat helps to avoid issue number one and makes them face their fears surrounding issue number two.

Steps are as follows:

1. Set an unloaded bar at the proper height to front squat. This will be at armpit height of the *shortest* lifter at that rack.

    Real world coaching note: The first thing that's going to happen is that athletes are 1000% going to stand back-to-back and argue to the death about who is 1/16 of an inch taller than the other. As the self-proclaimed chief of the no fun police, I address this before we start by saying: "this doesn't need to turn into a 15-minute 'I'M TALLER' battle conducted on tippy-toes. If two of you are so close in height that you need to measure, then it doesn't matter."

Anywho...rather than rely on them to accurately determine if the bar is actually at armpit height, I have the shortest lifter put their arm over the bar so that it nests in their armpit. If they can't do so *comfortably*, the bar is too high.

Front Squat Setup (Arm Over Bar)

"But the taller lifters will need to squat down!" That is correct. A taller lifter having to squat down is much safer than a shorter lifter trying to unrack the bar on their toes. Arrange your lifting groups by height when possible so it doesn't present that much of an issue.

2. Now that the bar is set to an appropriate height, we will teach athletes where the bar will be supported on the shoulders. Have the athletes extend their right arm out in front of them so that the arm is parallel to the floor, with the palm facing inward and the thumb pointing up. Using their left hand, feel for the groove on the front side of their right shoulder. This is where the bar will be placed.

Front Squat Setup (Find The Spot)

3. With the bar at the correct height, have the athlete line up facing the bar and instruct them to have their nose lined up *exactly* with the center of the bar. Do not assume they will know to line up here. I can assure you, they do not.

4. Walk forward until the front of the shoulders touch the bar.

5. Extend the arms out in front of the body underneath the bar, holding the palms in and thumbs up.

6. Unrack the bar with the bar resting on the front side of the shoulder, the groove they found earlier in step 2.

7. Walk a *half step* back from the rack. DO NOT ALLOW ATHLETES TO TAKE MULTIPLE STEPS BACK AWAY FROM THE RACK AND BELIEVE ME THEY WILL TRY. They should *always* be within the safety catches on the rack when squatting unless you are training Olympic weightlifters, which you most likely are not.

8. Set the feet, take a deep breath in, and brace the core.

9. Initiate the movement by sitting the hips back, ripping the floor apart with the feet.

10. The arms should remain parallel to the floor throughout the entire lift. What happens if they don't? Really simple: the bar rolls off their shoulders, providing immediate feedback via external cueing that the arms dropped. The athletes learn a few things here:
    a. The correct position for the arms during a front squat.
    b. That the hands don't have to death grip the bar in order to hold it in the front squat.

    c.   If the bar rolls off of their arms, the world doesn't screech to a halt. We are in the early stages of teaching them how to properly miss a front squat.

11. Be not afraid, you can–and should–add weight to the hands-free front squat as technique allows.

Hands Free BB Front Squat (Setup)

Hands Free BB Front Squat (Finish)

SQUAT PROGRESSION 4: THE BARBELL FRONT SQUAT

Despite having incorporated load during the hands-free barbell front squat, we will temporarily return to an empty bar while we learn the proper position in which to hold the bar for the front squat: the front rack position.

Steps are as follows:

1. Address the bar with the nose lined up in the center of the bar, exactly as they did in the hands-free squat.

2. Place the hands the same width the athlete uses for the RDL–a thumb's distance outside of the hips. Another way to locate this grip width is by placing the hands a thumb's distance away from the inside edge of the bar knurling or slightly wider, depending on comfort level. (For those

unfamiliar, knurling is the crosshatch pattern stamped into the barbell that allows for a more secure grip.)

3.   Rotate the elbows under the bar until the bar rests in the groove on the shoulders and the elbows are pointed straight ahead.

4.   The bar should be in the fingertips, not the palms of the hands. Some athletes may need to start with 1-2 fingers (pinky and ring finger) off of the bar to minimize wrist discomfort.

5.   Unrack the bar, take a *half step* back from the hooks, and squat.

BB Front Squat (Setup)

BB Front Squat (Finish)

A note on wrist discomfort: Many athletes will report this issue in the early stages of learning the front squat. This discomfort is typically due to trying to *grip* the bar with the hands, placing the wrist at an extreme angle. By simply teaching the athlete how to hold the bar on their shoulders versus with their hands, you will eliminate roughly 9 out of 10 complaints.

For athlete number 10, they may just need to acclimate to the position over the course of a few sessions. There also could be a legitimate mobility issue, like tight lats, preventing them from getting the elbows up; other possibilities would include a prior elbow or wrist injury, or a mobility issue in the wrist. Yes we want to work to address these issues, but in the meantime, we will need to modify the squat.

I don't allow athletes to use the crossed-arm position as an alternative. Instead, I attach lifting straps to the bar and have the athlete hold these straps with the elbows up. From my perspective, the crossed-arm position makes it more difficult to stay extended through the thoracic spine and makes it far more difficult to dump the bar in the event of a missed rep.

Rack Position Using Straps

On that note...your athletes shouldn't be missing reps. It may happen on very rare occasions, but that should be the exception rather than the rule. Too often, I see high school programs that are numbers driven and sacrifice technique and athlete safety in pursuit of the almighty 1 rep max. This is a dangerous and misguided practice. Our purpose is to develop better volleyball players, and poor technique will never transfer to the court.

However, don't misinterpret this as me saying not to lift heavy. Volleyball players should absolutely lift heavy when they can do so safely. Instead, I'm simply saying don't lift stupid.

Nonetheless, since the front squat is not an exercise that can be safely spotted, you do need to teach athletes how to miss in the event that they walked in and chose violence that day. Very simply, push the bar off the shoulders and push the body backwards and away from the bar, allowing the bar to crash onto the rack's safety arms.

A WORD ON TEMPO

While tempos can be used for any exercise, I find the method particularly useful when teaching the squat. I generally begin each new step of the teaching progression with a few weeks at a 3-2-1 tempo before progressing to a 5-2-1 tempo.

What does that mean? The numbers are seconds. The first is the eccentric portion (descent of the squat and most exercises), the second the isometric portion (bottom position), and the last is the concentric phase (the ascent).

So for a 3-2-1 tempo squat, they would squat down for three seconds, hold at the bottom for two, and spend one second coming back up. I just cue "come back up at a normal speed" because at this point I'm really only worried about control throughout the descent and owning the bottom position.

(Quick note to any pedantic Poliquin strength coaches who may be reading: ya, I realize there's a fourth number on a tempo indicating how long the movement should be locked out. That number is superfluous for 99% of the cases in which I'm using tempo, so I exclude it in my communication to athletes because it's one less thing for them to wrap their heads around.)

The reason I use tempo is so that athletes focus on controlling their entire range of motion, developing better eccentric strength as well as strength at the end range of the movement. End ranges are where athletes are generally the weakest and we want to make sure athletes are strong and stable across all ranges of motion required by the sport.

SQUAT FIX: THE SQUAT WEDGE

Generally speaking, you're going to see one of the following common squat errors:

1. The feet rotating out. This may be due to a lack of hip rotation or an inability to control it, and/or a lack of ankle mobility–specifically dorsiflexion. This often results in the knees caving inwards.

2. Excessive forward lean of the torso when trying to sit back.

3. Inability to achieve at least parallel depth.

If the cueing detailed in the various squat progressions above doesn't resolve these issues, my first step is to elevate the athlete's heels on a squat wedge. I have found this to be so effective at cleaning up common squat errors that I now teach all athletes the squat pattern using a wedge. Obviously, the wedge puts the athlete into a more knee-dominant squat pattern, but the goal is to eliminate use of the squat wedge within a few weeks for most athletes once they demonstrate the ability to do so. I generally start them with their entire foot on a 15 degree wedge, and have them put less and less of their foot on the wedge as they're able.

Front Squat on Wedge (Setup)

Front Squat on Wedge (Finish)

Some athletes, however, may never be able to take the wedge out of the equation due to severe mobility limitations. In this situation, I will typically give these athletes an alternative exercise–like a single leg movement–instead of a squat. Not every exercise fits every athlete, just like not every volleyball offense or defense fits every team. Do what is best for the athlete in front of you. Single-leg movements will be covered in the next chapter.

CHAPTER FOUR:
SINGLE-LEG MOVEMENTS

In both research and practice, single-leg movements have proven highly effective and broadly applicable for athletes, yet are often under-utilized in traditional strength and conditioning programs that heavily emphasize the "Big Three": the back squat, bench press, and conventional deadlift.

I categorize single-leg movements as either:

- *Hip dominant* = the shin angle is neutral to slightly positive, i.e., the knee stays roughly above the ankle in the front leg.
- *Knee dominant* = the shin angle is positive, i.e., the knee travels over the toe.

There are applications for both. However, since athletes tend to already be relatively knee dominant, I start by teaching hip-dominant variations, and these will be the focus of this chapter.

Also, before going any further, let's clarify terminology:

- Split squats–the athlete begins in a split stance and the feet do not displace during the movement.
- Lunges–the athlete begins with the feet together, steps into a split stance, and either returns to the start or travels in the direction of the lunge before starting the next rep.

BASICS OF HIP-DOMINANT SINGLE-LEG MOVEMENTS

1. The entire front foot should remain in contact with the ground throughout the movement.

2. The weight should be evenly distributed across the front foot.

3. The length of the stance should allow the athlete's knee to be directly above or slightly in front of the ankle at the bottom position of the lunge.

4. The torso should be relatively vertical with the shoulders stacked above the hips. The hips will be above or slightly in front of the back knee.

SPLIT SQUAT PROGRESSION 1: THE ISOMETRIC SPLIT SQUAT

Though split squats and lunges are both "top-down" exercises, I begin the first two steps in the teaching progression from a position of stability: the ground. This "bottom-up" approach allows athletes to focus on proper alignment and stride length before adding in the element of balance.

Steps are as follows:

1. Begin in a half-kneeling position. The front leg should be far enough in front of the body that the shin angle is neutral or slightly positive, meaning that the knee is positioned above or slightly in front of the ankle, but not over the toes.

2. "Load" the back toe by dorsiflexing the foot where it is perpendicular to the ground. Many young athletes will try to put their weight on the shoelaces of their back foot. This is an issue I'll likely never understand, but merits mentioning because it's very common.

3. Orient the torso perpendicular to the ground, with the shoulders stacked directly above the hips. The hips should be above or slightly in front of the back knee.

4. Position the arms wherever comfortable, as long as they are not resting on the front thigh or knee to "assist" the movement. Most athletes prefer the hands-on-hips position.

5. Initiate the movement by lifting the back knee off the ground. If a mirror is available, I cue athletes to see no change in the level of their head. If a mirror is not available, I tell them they should position their back knee so that their volleyball kneepad touches the floor, but they aren't resting on it. These are both slight over-exaggerations, but these external cues tend to produce better positioning than "stay low."

6. Hold this position for the prescribed amount of time. (I generally begin with 10 seconds with each leg and progress up to 30 seconds with each leg.)

Isometric Split Squat (Setup)

Isometric Split Squat (Finish)

SPLIT SQUAT PROGRESSION 2: THE BOTTOM-UP SPLIT SQUAT

In this step we begin to incorporate movement, but still begin the exercise from the floor. Steps are as follows:

1. Begin in a tall kneeling position, exactly the same as during iso split squats.

2. Stand up from the tall kneeling position until the top position of a split squat is reached, with the legs relatively straight.

3. Return to the starting position under control.

4. Come to rest in the tall kneeling position and repeat the movement.

Bottom-Up Split Squat (Setup)

Bottom-Up Split Squat (Finish)

SPLIT SQUAT PROGRESSION 3: THE ECCENTRIC TOP-DOWN SPLIT SQUAT

By this point, athletes should have an understanding of an appropriate stride length and be able to maintain balance. We will now begin to emphasize the eccentric phase of the exercise using an extended tempo. This extended tempo is valuable for a number of reasons, but here I use it to avoid being witness to a live-action rendition of Bambi on ice. As adorable as I find this classic movie scene, I prefer to avoid hearing kneecaps crashing into the floor as athletes self-select maximum velocity as their eccentric tempo.

Steps are as follows:

1. Begin in the top position of a split squat.

2. Descend towards the bottom position on a count of 3 to 6 seconds.

3. Lightly touch the knee to the floor to ensure a full range of motion.

4. Return to the top position.

This is the stage at which I will begin incorporating load, generally holding either one dumbbell in the goblet position, one dumbbell in the hand opposite the front leg, or two dumbbells held at the sides.

Eccentric Top-Down Split Squat (Setup)

Eccentric Top-Down Split Squat (Finish)

SPLIT SQUAT PROGRESSION 4A: THE REAR FOOT ELEVATED SPLIT SQUAT

Let's talk about equipment first.

- *Ideal*: a dedicated rear foot elevated station, aka rotating utility pad set up at about the level of the top third of an athlete's shin.
- *Good*: a box or bench that can be adjusted to the above height relative to an athlete's shin.
- *If you absolutely have to*: a box or bench of a fixed height. (The workaround here is to use a thicker bumper plate or small box/DC Block placed under the front foot to elevate the athlete to an appropriate height relative to the bench.)

I'll be describing this using a rotating utility pad, but extrapolate to fit your equipment.

Steps are as follows:

1. Stand in front of the pad, facing away from it.

2. Place the shoelaces of the rear foot over the pad.

3. The stride length generally feels slightly shorter than the previously described split squat, but the shin should remain neutral to slightly positive–meaning, the knee stays slightly in front of the front ankle, but not over the front toes.

4. The torso angle should roughly mirror the shin angle.

5. Descend under control until the front thigh is parallel to the ground, then return to the starting position.

6. Keep the front foot flat on the floor throughout the exercise.

Rear Foot Elevated Split Squat (Setup)

Rear Foot Elevated Split Squat (Finish)

I generally prefer to load this using either one dumbbell or a kettlebell held in the hand opposite the front leg, or with two dumbbells held at the sides.

Common errors in setup:

- The athlete is unable to keep the spine/pelvis neutral (aka an arch in the low back) = the pad or bench is too high for the athlete.
- The athlete's back knee touches the ground = the pad or bench is too low for the athlete.

SPLIT SQUAT PROGRESSION 4B: THE FRONT RACK BARBELL SPLIT SQUAT

Take a moment to revisit Chapter 3, progression 5: the barbell front squat. If athletes have mastered the front rack position and split squat progressions 1-3, you will have no difficulty at all teaching this movement. If they haven't mastered these prerequisites? Don't prescribe this exercise. I can assure you, if they aren't comfortable in the front rack position and you try to use it during single leg work... disaster is imminent.

Assuming proficiency, though...

1. Hold the barbell in the front rack position.

2. Begin in the top position of the split squat.

3. Descend, under control, until the back knee lightly touches the floor.

4. Return to the top position and repeat.

Front Rack BB Split Squat (Setup)

Front Rack BB Split Squat (Finish)

SINGLE-LEG PROGRESSION 5: REVERSE LUNGES

Lunges add another degree of difficulty due to having to move in and out of a proper stride length. As a result, I include them after an athlete has already spent a significant amount of time successfully performing split squats.

Although the forward lunge is traditionally used in programming, I favor the reverse lunge. Why? Because forward lunges tend to be more quad dominant, along with placing more strain on the anterior knee than reverse lunges. Not exactly what we're after in a sport that already places quite a bit of stress on this area. Anecdotally, my N of ~1,674 study using the reverse lunge over the forward lunge has produced relatively few "coach my knees are bad, I can't do these" complaints over the years.

Steps are as follows:

1. Stand with the feet hip distance apart.

2. Step the right leg backwards a distance that allows a neutral to slightly positive shin angle. This will be the same stride length as the split squat.

3. Descend under control, so that the back knee lightly touches the ground.

4. Return to start.

5. Alternate legs.

Reverse Lunge (Finish)

I generally prefer to load this one of three ways:

- One dumbbell held goblet style.
- Two dumbbells held at the sides.
- Barbell–front rack position or high bar position (on the back).

CHAPTER FIVE:
THE PUSH-UP

A few things make me angry in life: my extraordinary ability to shank a pass coming directly at my platform in serve receive and coaches who think athletes should just be able to drop and crank out a dozen military-grade push-ups, so they aren't taught or progressed. I have yet to be able to solve the first of these two problems, but this chapter should solve the second.

But first, why so much emphasis on a well-executed push-up? Why not just bench press? The push-up has benefits that extend well beyond just upper body strength. While upper body strength is important for a volleyball player to be able generate a powerful arm swing, they must do so by utilizing:

1. Core stability

2. Scapular movement

3. Scapular stability

While the bench press isn't really that great at checking any of those boxes, a well-executed push-up checks all three.

BASICS OF THE PUSH-UP

1. Keep the body in a straight line from head to heels throughout the entire range of motion. The core should be tight and the glutes and quads squeezed.

2. "Pack" the neck so that the chin remains neutral and the head is still, just as in all previous movements.

3. Keep the elbows at 45-degree angles from the body and NEVER flare out wide.

4. Complete a full range of motion. This means chest to the floor or to a target a few inches above the floor (like a dome cone, 1" thick bumper plate, etc.). The rep should be fully locked out so that both the triceps and the serratus anterior (both important muscles for scapular movement and stability) are engaged.

PUSH-UP PROGRESSION 0: TEACHING THE PELVIC TILT

This is a beneficial skill to teach before beginning any other movement. But, I'm five chapters in and not interested in restructuring this book; also, I'm generally teaching the first step in each movement progression at the same time, so just because the pelvic tilt isn't included on the front end of this book, that doesn't mean it doesn't get taught in an athlete's first few sessions. It does.

There are a number of ways to teach the pelvic tilt, but I prefer to teach it in the glute bridge position.

1. Lie face up on the floor with the arms about 45 degrees from the sides and the palms flat on the floor.

2. Bend the knees so that the feet are flat on the floor and hip distance apart.

3. "Peel" the tailbone off of the floor so that the pelvis tilts posteriorly.

4. Return to the start and repeat.

Glute Bridge (Setup)

Glute Bridge (Finish)

From here, we will begin the 2-part glute bridge:

1. Peel the tailbone off the floor.

2. Maintain this pelvic tilt and drive the hips off of the floor until the body is a straight line from the knees to the shoulders. We do not want to see a "dip" at the hips from a lack of full hip extension, nor do we want to see a "bubble" caused by lumbar hyperextension instead of hip extension.

3. If you want two different variations:
    a. Keep the feet flat and drive the big-toe into the floor for greater glute engagement.
    b. Lift the toes off the ground with the weight on the heels for more hamstring engagement.

Once athletes have a feel for this neutral pelvic positioning and have demonstrated an ability to maintain it during a glute bridge, I start the push-up progression from the top of the movement down.

PUSH-UP PROGRESSION 1: THE HIGH PLANK

This is an often overlooked step in teaching the push-up, but one that I believe is important as it trains a neutral pelvis and core stability in the specific position required to complete a push-up.

To complete the high plank:

1. Begin at the top of a push-up position. The palms should be flat on the floor with the fingertips forward and the hands shoulder distance apart or slightly wider.

2. The body should be a straight line from head to heels, with the head neutral so that the eyes look between the hands or slightly in front.

3. Complete a pelvic tilt and hold this position by contracting the quads and glutes along with bracing the core.

4. Hold this position for time. I usually start at 20 seconds and progress to as much as 60 seconds.

High Plank

For athletes who lack upper body strength, the high plank alone will provide a stimulus to strengthen the arms while simultaneously improving core strength and stability.

PUSH-UP PROGRESSION 2: THE ECCENTRIC PUSH-UP

Many developmental athletes will not have the requisite core and upper body strength to complete a full range of motion push-up. They can, however, be quite successful completing the eccentric portion of the movement providing they receive proper instruction. By focusing on this portion of the movement, we allow athletes to ingrain the proper movement pattern while simultaneously developing the strength to complete their first full ROM push-up at a later date.

Steps are as follows:

1. Start in the high plank position in a straight line from head to heels with the arms fully locked out.

2. Descend slowly for 3-6 seconds, keeping the arms at 45-degree angles away from the body and maintaining a straight line from head to heels. Do not allow the elbows to flare away from the body or the low back or head to sag.

3. Lower until the chest touches and rests on the floor.

4. Return to the starting position using one of the following methods, based on the athlete's current ability:
    a. Ideal return to start: the athlete pushes themselves up to the top position using perfect form (*spoiler*

alert: this won't happen for most until they have many sessions under their belt).

b. Good return to start: the athlete uses the knees to assist the push-up, but maintains a neutral spine (straight line from head to knees).

c. WIT: *whatever it takes* return to start–let them return to start in whatever manner they are able to.

Eccentric Push-Up

Common errors at this point will be allowing the low back to sag (lumbar hyperextension) or flaring the elbows. If cueing the athlete doesn't solve the issue, elevate the hands onto a bench, box, or barbell so they are supporting less of their body weight and maintaining proper alignment.

As with any exercise or lift, technique is the number one priority. Not only is this important for injury reduction, it also ensures that the muscles and movement patterns used will have better transfer to the sport.

PUSH-UP PROGRESSION 3: HANDS-ELEVATED PUSH-UP

As described in the previous step, elevating the hands allows the athlete to complete push-ups with less of their body weight. While elevating the hands certainly changes the movement pattern, the idea is to decrease the height of the box or bench over time so that the athlete's hands are eventually on the floor.

1. Find a box or bench height that allows the athlete to maintain proper alignment in the spine and elbows throughout the entire range of motion. The box/bench should be of adequate width to allow the same hand placement as in previous steps.

2. Begin in the top position, with the arms locked and the body in a straight line from head to heels.

3. Lower the body, under control, until the chest touches the box/bench.

4. Press the body away from the bench, ensuring that the head, hips, and heels remain in a straight line and the elbows remain approximately 45 degrees away from the body.

Hands Elevated Push-Up (Setup)

Hands Elevated Push Up (Finish)

If an athlete is unable to maintain proper alignment, increase the height of the box or bench.

PUSH-UP PROGRESSION 4: HAND-RELEASE PUSH-UP

Having established what proper alignment feels like, we will begin working from the ground up. (You can skip this step if you determined in step 3 that your athlete is able to do full range of motion push-ups with their hands on the floor.)

1. Start in the bottom position of the push-up, with the hands shoulder distance or slightly wider and the elbows no wider than a 45-degree angle from the torso.

2. Load the toes–meaning the feet are dorsiflexed.

3. Begin in proper alignment by initiating a pelvic tilt, bracing the core, and squeezing the glutes and quads.

4. Lift the hands off the floor, then place them back down and drive the body off the floor, maintaining the straight line from head to heels.

5. Finish with the arms fully locked out, then press the chest further away from the floor in order to move the scapula into protraction, engaging the serratus anterior.

6. Lower the body back to the floor under control, lift the hands, and repeat.

Hand Release Push-Up (Setup)

Hand Release Push-Up (Finish)

PUSH-UP PROGRESSION 5: PUSH-UPS AND PUSH-UP VARIATIONS

By this point, the athlete should be able to complete a full range of motion push-up, maintaining proper alignment at all times. In case you fell asleep in steps 1-4, that means we see none of the following common errors:

1. The low back sagging due to lumbar hyperextension.

2. The head sagging.

3. Forward head posture (the dreaded chin poke).

4. The elbows flaring out wide.

5. Not attaining full depth (chest not touching the floor).

6. Failure to lock out.

With those technique flaws banished as ghosts of weight rooms past, you should be able to incorporate most push-up variations into your program. What's my personal favorite? So glad you asked.

The Push-Up to Shoulder Tap:

Beyond the push-up, this is an anti-rotation exercise for the core.

1. Begin at the top position of a push-up.

2. Place the feet slightly wider than shoulder distance apart. It is important to understand that the wider the feet are, the less difficult it is to stay square during this exercise. The more narrow the feet, the more it will challenge the ability of the core to resist rotation. Use the foot placement that works for each athlete. Do not advance them beyond what they are able to control.

3. Lower the chest to the floor under control and immediately return to the top position.

4. Once the arms are locked out, lift the right hand off the floor and touch it to the left shoulder.

5. Do not allow the hips to rotate.

6. Pause with the hand on the left shoulder for two seconds, then replace the hand back on the ground.

7. Lift the left hand and place it on the right shoulder for two seconds without allowing the hips to rotate. Place the hand back on the ground.

8. Begin a second push-up.

Push-Up to Shoulder Tap (Setup)

Push-Up to Shoulder Tap (Finish)

FINAL PUSH-UP THOUGHTS

Real talk: push-ups are hard, particularly for athletes with long limbs (as volleyball players often are). The rate at which they move through these steps will likely vary more than any other exercise we've covered so far in this book. Often, I've had athletes who can do 2-3 phenomenal push-ups, then they fall apart.

So how do I handle it if the program I wrote on the whiteboard says they have a set of 8?!

I am completely fine with them doing as many *perfect* push-ups as they can, then taking a step back to a hand release push-up or even a hands-elevated push-up to finish the remaining reps in the set. Always meet your athletes where they are at, not where you think they should be that day.

CHAPTER SIX:
UPPER BODY PULLING

Due to the overwhelming importance of upper body pulling in shoulder health for a volleyball athlete, this chapter will outline two key variations:

1.   Horizontal pulling via the reverse pull-up (aka inverted row).

2.   Vertical pulling via the chin-up.

Coaches and athletes must understand that in the sport of volleyball, the ability to stabilize the scapula has direct implications on the health of the shoulder. Too often, because of a heavy emphasis on the bench press and its variants, I see strength and conditioning programs that are biased in the direction of the front side of the shoulder by having more pressing movements/sets/reps—or, *even worse*, I see programs that are missing pulling movements entirely.

This is a very risky game to play–particularly in an era where athletes spend an overabundance of time hunched over their phones, laptops, or homework. The net effect of these postures is the creation of tightness in the front side of the shoulder and weakness in the back side, where the muscles that stabilize the scapulae reside. Add into this the facts that volleyball demands a rounded, kyphotic posture during passing and defense and places tremendous stress on the shoulder when serving and attacking and you have a recipe for disaster if the musculature of the upper back is not properly trained.

A good rule of thumb is to try to maintain a 2:1 ratio of upper body pulling to upper body pressing. If this means that due to time constraints you need to sacrifice some upper body pressing? Then sacrifice some upper body pressing. The last thing your program needs is for your 6 rotation starter with a whip for an arm to be sitting on the bench because there "wasn't enough time" to include a sufficient amount of upper body pulls. Remember the wise words of my husband: *we find time for the things that are important to us*. Shoulder health? Pretty important to us in the volleyball world.

Another real world training tip you won't see in many books: when you're calculating your pull:push ratio, you also need to include the push-ups you're using in practice for punishment. That math can be daunting, so here's a fool-proof formula that will assist: stop using push-ups as punishment (or, for that matter, any exercise). You're a better coach than that or you wouldn't be here reading this book.

HORIZONTAL PULLING BASICS: THE REVERSE PULL-UP

The reverse pull-up can very simply be described as taking the body position in the hands-elevated push-up and flipping it on its back!

1. Set a barbell up in a rack at approximately the height of the athlete's xiphoid process (lowest point of the sternum).

2. Sitting with the hips underneath the bar should set the feet up in the correct position for the pull.

3. Place a bench, box, or bumper plate in front of the athlete so the feet can be braced against it.

4. Grip the bar with the palms facing up toward the ceiling so the shoulders are externally rotated, hands shoulder distance apart.

5. Lift the hips off the ground so the body is in a straight line from the head to the heels. Complete a posterior pelvic tilt, bracing the core and contracting the glutes to ensure that the hips do not sag towards the floor or that the back doesn't arch.

6. The head should remain neutral with the neck packed.

7. During the movement, retract and depress the scapulae– meaning, pull the shoulder blades together and down during the ascent towards the bar. Allow the shoulder blades to return to their initial, protracted position during the descent.

While scapular stability is important, the athlete's scapulae must also be trained to move appropriately. In horizontal rowing variations, incorrect movement of the scapula is relatively easy to spot. Instead of the chest being out and the shoulders remaining down, an athlete with incorrect pulling mechanics will finish with the shoulders forward and shrugged up towards their ears. The result of allowing this movement pattern to persist will be an imbalance between the upper and lower traps, which puts the shoulder at risk due to an inability of the scapula to function properly during overhead movement.

8. To reiterate, the shoulders should finish back and down, but also with the elbows finishing only slightly behind the body. When athletes finish with the shoulders forward and the elbows well behind their body, they are using humeral hyperextension versus scapular retraction to complete the movement. Humeral hyperextension places a great deal of unnecessary strain on the anterior shoulder capsule along with moving the shoulder blade into posterior tilt, the exact opposite of what is required for the arm to move overhead.

9. The bar should finish around the height of the base of the sternum (xiphoid process), or for those wearing sports bras, at about the height of the band.

Reverse Pull-Up (Setup: with hips under bar)

Reverse Pull-Up (Setup: Bottom Position)

Reverse Pull-Up (Finish: Top Position)

Reverse Pull-Up (Common Error: Humeral Hyperextension)

REVERSE PULL-UP PROGRESSION 1: ISOMETRIC REVERSE PULL-UP

We will begin this progression by first ensuring that the athlete is able to maintain proper alignment in the end range position of the reverse pull-up.

Steps are as follows:

1. The set-up is the same as above.

2. Begin at the top position of the movement, where the body is in contact with the bar and the scapulae are retracted and depressed. A good cue for scapular depression is *put your shoulder blades into your back pockets*. This will eliminate the tendency to shrug the shoulders towards the ears. *Ears are shoulder poison* –which I stole from an unknown source–has proved a popular cue with athletes.

3. Ensure that the body remains in a straight line from head to heels. If the hips are sagging towards the ground, it is often due to rounding the shoulders forward to reach the bar versus retracting the shoulder blades to reach the bar. Alternatively, we don't want to see an excessive arch in the low back in an attempt to reach the bar.

4. Hold this top position for time. I generally start athletes at around 10-15 seconds and progress to 30 seconds.

5. For athletes unable to hold this top position, simply raise the height of the bar (and adjust whatever they are bracing their feet against) just as you would raise the height of the box during hands-elevated push-ups. This requires athletes to support less of their body weight, so they are able to progress at the pace that works for them. It is unwise to allow a struggling athlete to complete reps with poor technique and believe that it will get better as they get stronger. They will get stronger, but not at the intended movement. Instead, they will become better at compensating with aberrant movement patterns, which over time can lead to injury on the court.

REVERSE PULL-UP PROGRESSION 2: ECCENTRIC REVERSE PULL-UP

By this point, you may have observed a trend in several of the teaching progressions: moving from an isometric to an eccentric emphasis, and then on to more dynamic movements. The reverse pull-up progression will follow this pattern as well. Like the push-up, many developmental athletes will lack the requisite upper body strength to complete the entire range of motion using the desired movement pattern and corresponding musculature, but can still be successful with this eccentric variant.

Steps are as follows:

1. The set-up is the same as above.

2. Begin at the top of the movement, with the body close to the bar and the shoulder blades retracted, keeping the shoulders away from the ears.

3. Descend for a count of 3-6 seconds, focusing on moving from the scapula throughout the entire range of motion. The descent should be smooth. Some athletes will show a "pulse" in the movement at each second. This is simply a lack of understanding of what is being asked. An explanation to be smooth during the descent will easily rectify this situation.

4. Return to the top position in any way necessary and repeat.

REVERSE PULL-UP PROGRESSION 3: 2-COUNT PAUSE REVERSE PULL-UP

Following along with the trend outlined in progression number 2, we progress to a more dynamic movement.

Steps are as follows:

1. Set-up the same as above, this time beginning at the bottom of the movement with the arms fully extended and the body in a straight line from head to heels.

2. With the core braced and the glutes contracted, begin to pull the body up towards the bar, focusing on retracting and depressing the shoulder blades and keeping the elbows tucked into the sides.

3. Hold the top position for a 2-count before descending, under control, to the starting position.

Two notes here:

1. Tempo is one of the areas in sports where there seems to be a language barrier between coach and athlete.

   Coach says: "2-count pause at the top."

   Coach means: 1-Mississippi-2-Mississippi.

   Athlete hears: "Slam my chest into the bar and drop like a rock to the bottom?

   NAILED IT."

It's a tale as old as time. To solve this in a team setting, I often have the group count out loud with me prior to starting the exercise to get a feel for the desired tempo. Then, I have athletes paired in groups of three. Assignments are as follows:

Athlete 1: Completing the primary movement (in this case reverse pull-up).

Athlete 2: Completing an auxiliary movement.

Athlete 3: Coaching Athlete 1, including holding them accountable to tempo.

2. This step in the reverse pull-up progression is usually the stage at which we start to see athletes attempting to do "the worm" in order to complete the movement. Since they should already understand the parameters of the movement given the fact they have demonstrated correct body positioning in the steps leading up to this point, this unsolicited breakdance move likely represents a strength deficit. Raise the height of the bar until they can complete the exercise properly. This may mean the bar is placed higher than it was during earlier steps in the progression. That's okay. When we change one criteria (adding the concentric portion of the exercise), we often have to relax the previous criteria (the height of the bar) in order to ensure success. What we never relax is our demand for quality movement patterns.

REVERSE PULL-UP PROGRESSION 4: PARTNER-RESISTED ECCENTRIC REVERSE PULL-UP

The most commonly understood way to progress any exercise is by adding load. However, with an exercise like the reverse pull-up, this can be challenging to do unless you have a large number of weight vests at your disposal (which you probably do not). What you may have at your disposal is a large number of athletes standing around ready to be put to work, because the session is structured with athletes in groups of three as outlined in the previous step.

The steps that follow will describe this activity as it relates to Athletes 1 and 3 in the group. (Recall that Athlete 2 will be completing an unrelated auxiliary exercise.)

1. Athlete 1 will set up at the bottom position of the reverse pull-up.

2. Athlete 3 should be positioned so they can put their hand on Athlete 1's shoulder or above their chest.

3. Athlete 1 will pull to the top of the movement by retracting and depressing the shoulder blades.

4. Athlete 3 will then try to push Athlete 1 away from the bar. Expect to spend more time coaching Athlete 3 to challenge Athlete 1 than vice versa.

5. Athlete 1 will resist Athlete 3's push so that the descent is 3-6 seconds in length.

6. Athlete 1 will then return to the top unresisted by Athlete 3.

Reverse Pull-Up (Partner Resisted Eccentric)

VERTICAL PULLING BASICS: THE NEUTRAL GRIP CHIN-UP

First, let's talk verbiage: chin-ups versus pull-ups.

Chin-up = the grip is either supinated (underhand) or neutral (palms facing each other). Generally, the hands are placed shoulder distance apart.

Pull-up = the grip is pronated (overhand). Generally, the hands are placed outside of shoulder distance.

This section will discuss the chin-up, which I find to be the more shoulder-friendly option of the two, along with being more achievable for most athletes. Here are the chin-up's basic principles:

1. Most racks will have a chin-up bar of some type. Whether or not your set-up has a dual grip option with the neutral grips may dictate your choice between neutral and supinated. If given the option, I will primarily choose neutral grip with my athletes as it puts their shoulders and elbows in a position that "feels" better to most athletes.

    For shorter athletes who have difficulty reaching the bar and where climbing up the rack isn't safe, help them raise the barbell to a height on the rack that they can reach. Optimally, it is at a height that their feet don't touch the ground at the bottom, but your rack may not allow that so have them tuck their knees to avoid standing on the ground.

Chin-Up (Setup: for smaller athletes)

2. Grip the bar with a closed grip–meaning, the thumb is on the opposite side of the bar of the fingers. Do not use a "false" grip.

3. Come to a dead-hang position where the arms and shoulders are fully extended.

4. Ensure that the spine is neutral by completing a pelvic tilt and bracing the core.

5. Pull-up towards the bar by driving the shoulder blades down and keeping the chest up/out throughout the movement.

6. Just as in horizontal pulling variations, do not allow the shoulders to round forward in order to make contact with the bar.

7. When the end range of motion is reached (chest near the bar), descend to the starting position under control. The elbows should be fully extended prior to beginning the next rep.

CHIN-UP PROGRESSION 1: THE STRAIGHT ARM HANG WITH OVERCOMING ISOMETRIC

For some, in the early stages of learning, simply hanging from the bar may be a challenge due to a lack of upper body strength, grip strength, or both. A starting point for these athletes may be to straight arm hang for 10 seconds and progress to where they can hang for 30 seconds.

Once the athlete has reached this 30-second milestone, begin incorporating "overcoming isometrics." This means exerting force against an immovable object–in this case, the athlete's own body weight. The overcoming isometric may look different for each athlete in the room. Some may remain virtually motionless despite exerting a maximal attempt to pull-up, while others may be able to pull themselves partially to the top. Still others may figure out they already have the requisite strength to complete their first pull-up!

This is actually a great informal assessment for you as a coach, and one where you can safely allow athletes to give maximal effort from day one, teaching the skill of strain.

At any rate, wherever they finish their overcoming isometric, hold this position for 5 seconds, descend back to start, and repeat for 1-3 reps. They may have to drop off the bar in between reps and that's okay! It is CRITICAL that the athletes not see an inability to pull part or all of the way up as a failure, rather just a step in the process. Praise their effort and improvement.

CHIN-UP PROGRESSION 2: TOP POSITION ISOMETRIC CHIN-UP

In the same phase of training, I will incorporate isometrics in the top position to ingrain the pattern of chest out, shoulder blades back and down so that we later don't see chest caved and shoulders rounded forward to meet the bar.

Steps are as follows:

1. Pull or hop to the top position of a chin-up*. Hold the top position with the shoulders back and down.

2. Ensure that the spine is neutral.

3. Hold this position for 10-30 seconds.

4. Athletes unable to hold for this length of time can hold as many seconds as they are able, then without dropping off the bar, descend into the bottom position and hold in a straight arm hang.

*As a reminder, it may be necessary from a safety perspective to modify the rack set-up for shorter athletes. Rather than use the chin-up bar itself, you can set the barbell at a height that they can reach either standing, on their tippy-toes, or using a small hop. The splat that occurs when an athlete hits the floor during a chin-up related crash is a sound you'll never unhear. Which reminds me, I need to order some chalk for my facility, and you should too. Regardless of whether you're using a barbell or the rack's chin-up bar, clammy hands make for slippery grips.

Chin-Up (Finish: Top Position)

CHIN-UP PROGRESSION 3: ECCENTRIC CHIN-UPS

No curveball here, the next step in our progression will be an eccentric emphasis. Steps are as follows:

1. Pull or hop to the top position of the chin-up with the shoulders back and down and the spine neutral.

2. Descend to the bottom position for the prescribed amount of time. I usually begin with reps of 10 seconds, increasing 2-5 seconds per week depending on athlete readiness

until the 30 second mark is reached. Generally speaking, once an athlete can do a 30-second controlled eccentric, they can do their first unassisted chin-up. Even if that's not entirely true...if you tell them it is, they will do their first chin-up. I once gaslit an athlete into believing that she could do one more chin-up each week than she had the week before. By week 12 of the season? Guess what... she did 12 chin-ups. At 6'2"! An outlier story to be sure, but the point remains–*athletes rise to the demands of their environment.*

3. Upon reaching the bottom, pull or jump back to the top position and begin the next rep.

Since you will likely have a wide array of strength levels in the group, but may not have the capacity to execute multiple different steps in the progression, you can challenge the handful of stronger athletes who are unphased by the prescribed amount of time by having them perform weighted eccentrics by wearing a weighted chin-up belt or weight vest. For the handful of athletes in the opposite situation– unable to maintain control for the duration of the set–they can hold a straight arm hang for the remaining time. For a set of 15 seconds, this might look like an athlete descending for 7 seconds, then holding a straight arm hang for 8 seconds.

CHIN-UP PROGRESSION 4: ECCENTRIC CHIN-UPS WITH OVERCOMING ISOMETRIC

To review: an overcoming isometric is a rep completed by exerting maximal effort against a load that the athlete cannot move. In this case, the athlete's body weight. Among a few other purposes, these can be used to help athletes develop the strength required to break through sticking points like the ones that would cause you to not be able to complete a full chin-up.

Steps are as follows:

1. Complete a 10-15 second eccentric chin-up as before.

2. When the bottom position is reached (arms near full extension), pull up with maximal effort for 5 seconds. Some athletes will hardly move. Others will move a few inches before reaching a point they cannot pass. Still others will mysteriously teleport to the top position of a chin-up to their great surprise and the coaches' delight. For this last group of athletes, go ahead and move them on to progression 5. This will boost their confidence! It will also likely result in several other athletes achieving their first full rep over the next couple of sessions: the chin-up version of Roger Bannister and breaking the barrier of the 4-minute mile.

3. Complete 2-3 reps.

Regardless of where an athlete falls along the spectrum, coaches need to make a point of praising effort over execution, as there will likely be a wide range of strength levels in the room.

CHIN-UP PROGRESSION 5: CHIN-UP

The expectations for this were outlined above in the vertical pulling basics section. But what happens when an athlete gets their first chin-up, but they can only do one rep? A couple of notes.

First, I keep my chin-up volume relatively low. Better a few sets of 2-3 outstanding reps than a set of 6-8 poorly executed. Quality beats quantity.

Next, let's say I've programmed a set of 3 chin-ups, but the athlete can only do 1 chin-up. They will finish out the set with two 5-10 second eccentric + 5 second overcoming isometric chin-ups. The idea being that after a few sessions, it becomes 2 chin-ups + 1 ecc/overcoming iso, then 3 + 0, then 4, and so on. Not every athlete will be in the same place on any given day, so it is important to have easy-to-implement plans in place that accommodate for different rates of progression.

CHIN-UP PROGRESSION 6: WEIGHTED CHIN-UP

A simple progression for the few athletes who are no longer challenged by the prescribed rep scheme is to add weight via a weighted pull-up belt or weight vest.

CHAPTER SEVEN:
CLOSING THOUGHTS ON BASIC MOVEMENT PATTERNS AND PROGRESSIONS

Prior to moving on from these basic training progressions, I want to clarify two points.

1. THINGS DON'T JUST DISAPPEAR

You might see the steps within each movement pattern as a linear progression where the previous step is never used again once mastered, but that isn't the case. Instead of looking at it as a series of exercises to zip through on the way to the top, understand that there are a number of scenarios when a particular variation of a movement may be the best choice, even if an athlete has mastered higher steps in the progression.

Here are a few reasons we would revisit various steps in a progression:

1. An athlete, despite previous mastery of a movement, shows up one day having experienced–or is currently experiencing–a growth spurt. What was easy yesterday is proving challenging today as they adjust to altered limb length and center of mass. By having a system in place to teach movements, we can quickly adapt to the needs of an athlete without rewriting an entire training program.

2. Managing fatigue in-season. Sometimes, I'll program less taxing movements (like a goblet squat instead of a barbell front squat) or isometrics (which decrease the chances of being sore from the weight room to just around zero due to eliminating the eccentric stress of a movement). These simple modifications can help us manage athlete stress and soreness in-season without feeling compelled to mysteriously lose our keys to the weight room and not darken the door again until after the season is over.

Also, while this book primarily targets athletes looking to become college-ready, even collegiate and professional athletes utilize most of these basic exercises and progressions in their own training programs. For professional and elite level athletes, their number one priority is fine-tuning the technical skills and tactical strategies that will pay their bills. This comes at an enormous cost from an energy standpoint, which often does not allow hours to be dedicated to cute little specialized exercises. Their training programs are often far more basic than social media would lead you to believe. In truth, there was nothing exceptionally advanced about how I trained Division I volleyball players. It was the basics, well-executed.

2. THERE'S MORE TO IT THAN JUST THESE EXERCISES...BUT

We really haven't addressed anything beyond the sagittal plane, when many sport movements and skills demand speed/power/strength in the frontal and transverse planes. But, if you understand the movement principles outlined thus far, you can extrapolate these principles to teaching most other exercises. Show me a movement I've never seen, and using only the principles outlined in this book, I would be able to teach it with a pretty high level of success.

That being said, if the only performance training a volleyball player ever does outside of their sport are the things contained in this book, they will be ahead of 95% of their peers ages 7-27 from an athletic development standpoint.

SECTION 2:
SPEED, PLYOMETRICS, CHANGE OF DIRECTION & CONDITIONING

Scan the QR Code to watch the Demo Videos that correspond with the Exercise Progressions and Images listed in Section 2:

Prior to starting these three chapters, I'd like to point out that the topics of speed, plyometrics/COD, and conditioning are *separate chapters*. This is because they are NOT the same thing. Speed is not conditioning. Plyometrics are not conditioning. Conditioning is conditioning. Coaches need to be careful not to conflate these elements of an athlete's training program by attempting to use one to develop the other.

Further, let's briefly revisit the Youth Physical Development Models in Chapter 1, pages 22-23 of this text. Where does metabolic conditioning fall in the realm of importance for developmental athletes? Well behind the other physical capacities. Yet many coaches place almost all of their emphasis on whether or not their volleyball athletes are "in shape" and then design workouts with the express purpose of inducing fatigue. This is not the purpose of conditioning workouts. The purpose of conditioning workouts is to develop the physiological adaptations that will support how many times and how often an athlete can repeat high intensity outputs, like maximal jumps, accelerations, and decelerations on the volleyball court. In order to be able to *repeat* a strength/power/speed output, one must first be able to *produce* one, so we will begin there.

CHAPTER EIGHT:
DEVELOPING SPEED

Speed wins games. Whether it's a libero pursuing a dig, a setter chasing an out-of-system pass, or an attacker getting their feet to the ball during an approach, speed is critical in volleyball.

However, much of the sport of volleyball is played in a 9 meter by 9 meter box, with 6 players each charged with covering an even smaller area. With that being the case, there is a tendency in the volleyball community to ignore the basic motor ability of speed due to a "lack of specificity." After all, we are training volleyball players, not track athletes!

If that's your mindset, please humor me for a moment and answer a few questions:

1. Would it benefit a volleyball athlete to increase the number of muscle fibers recruited during a movement? (Increased power outputs.)

2. Would it benefit a volleyball athlete to have a faster rate of force development? (Often defined as "first step quickness" or explosiveness, but really it's *how fast can you overcome inertia?*)

3. Would it benefit a volleyball athlete to have faster contract/relax cycles? (This is a differentiator between athletes who are smooth/fluid and ones who appear more robotic.)

4. Would improvements in general coordination benefit a volleyball athlete?

5. Did you read Chapter 1, where we discussed the importance of *general* athletic development as an enhancer of sport skill?

If you answered "yes" to *any* of those five questions, then we agree that sprinting, though on the surface not "sport specific," will have a high rate of transfer to the development of a volleyball player.

With that out of the way, let's look at a few principles that underlie speed development.

SPEED DEVELOPMENT PRINCIPLES

I'm going to steal these directly from my friend Tony Holler, the originator of the Feed the Cats training system. If you aren't familiar with his work, let me give you the Cliff's Notes.

Tony is a longtime high school coach and teacher who developed a speed training system based on the idea that training should develop high performing athletes who are fast and well-recovered, or "cats," instead of "dogs" who typically underperform due to being overworked in training. Due to its simplicity and effectiveness, his Feed the Cats system has been adopted by teams in every sport across the United States. Here are a few of his speed development mantras:

1. "Sprint as fast as possible, as often as possible, while staying as fresh as possible."

    What does this mean? It means that in order to get fast, we have to train fast. Where lifting at submaximal intensities will lead to gains in strength, running at submaximal speeds trains the body to move at submaximal speed. Speed sessions need to be conducted at 95%+ intensity, which means not only are athletes not fatigued coming into the session, they shouldn't become fatigued *during* the session. One way to ensure this is to allow adequate rest between reps.

    A good rule of thumb is that for every 10 yards/meters sprinted, there should be 30-60 seconds of recovery before starting the next rep. One caveat here is that when using

10 yard accelerations, I don't time recoveries–instead, I roll my groups through, let them walk back, and line back up to start the next rep (usually I have athletes 3-4 deep in line, depending on the facility). Rarely are we hitting top speed or inducing fatigue at this distance, so the walk-back protocol, along with the natural rest of waiting their turn, should serve as sufficient recovery.

SPRINT DISTANCE	RECOVERY INTERVAL
10 yards	Walk back
20 yards	Walk back + 30 seconds
30 yards	Walk back + 60 seconds
40 yards	Walk back + 120 seconds

I seldom have my volleyball athletes sprint a distance longer than 30 yards. While there absolutely are benefits to touching maximal velocity, we aren't dealing with track and field athletes. Most team sport athletes reach top speed by 20-30 yards, and this holds even more true for younger athletes. Additionally, from a practical standpoint, volleyball players are often training in a gym with limited space and 30 yards is all that's available.

An added benefit of this is that *most* of the work done in the speed training of a volleyball player falls under the heading of acceleration work, which is easier for athletes to recover from than longer, maximal velocity sprints of 40 yards and beyond.

Regardless of the distance, when chasing gains in speed, ensure that you allow full recovery before completing the next rep. *Full transparency*: if you haven't ever coached a speed training session that allows for optimal recovery, the first time you do it's going to make you incredibly anxious to see more rest being completed than work. But...

Performance is more important than hard work.

Read that again. And ten more times as a lead in to the next Feed the Cats Principle:

2.   "Don't let today's session ruin tomorrow's session."

When planning training sessions for the week, structure them in a way that speed is prioritized on days that athletes are fresh. In other words, don't plan a speed session:

- On Monday after a club tournament that finished on Sunday.
- The day after a heavy conditioning session.
- The day after a heavy lower body lift.

Remember: fresh & fast.

3.   "It is better to be 100% healthy and 80% in shape than the opposite," aka "don't burn the steak."

This concept can be extrapolated across *all* facets of athlete development and is my favorite quote in all of sports performance. Training goal #1-1000 is to keep athletes healthy.

These above *principles* serve as the foundation for a good speed development program. Below are the *methods*.

SPEED DEVELOPMENT METHODS – DRILLS

Given the following:

- The heavy reliance on acceleration in the sport of volleyball.
- The space constraints that most volleyball training programs operate in.
- The ease of recoverability for acceleration versus maximal velocity work.
- The need to develop fluid mechanics with athletes.

One might then assume that volleyball athletes should solely focus on acceleration without worrying about top-end speed. This, however, is not the case. Acceleration improves an athlete's ability to reach a given speed sooner, but isn't necessarily moving the needle on what that speed is. But maximal velocity work will. So, if our objective is to produce faster athletes who can utilize that speed in a shorter time period, we need to train both. To phrase that a bit differently:

- Maximal Velocity = how fast are you?
- Acceleration = how fast can you be fast?

The good news—and an important principle—is that the mechanics of acceleration and the mechanics of maximal velocity are roughly the same. The primary difference is the direction that the force is applied (i.e., more horizontal force application during acceleration versus more vertical force application during maximal velocity).

With that, most of our technical drills will focus on the development of the "A-Position."

Some coaches will argue against the use of technical drills for speed, saying that the quality is self-organizing in nature and that efforts can be better focused elsewhere in the training process. Others will say we need to devote large volumes of time to perfecting speed mechanics. My stance lies right in the middle of the self-organization proponents and the drill enthusiasts.

We will spend a little time teaching athletes to run smoothly before expecting them to run fast. With time rarely on our side in a given training session, we must be as efficient as possible in our programming. Generally, incorporating 5-10 minutes of speed mechanics via A-Series drills at the end of or in place of a general dynamic warm-up will provide a sufficient stimulus for athletes without overtaking the entire training session.

When completing our drill work, we will follow the 80% guideline—meaning that the athlete will focus on completing drill work at 80% intensity. Surely this statement must raise an eyebrow after having just been told that running at anything less than 95%+ of maximal intensity will not be beneficial for speed development. This 80% method is used to avoid seeing athletes, who potentially haven't learned or don't understand the A-Position, end up looking like Phoebe running through Central Park in Season 6, Episode 7 of the classic Sitcom "Friends."

BASICS OF THE A-POSITION

1. 3 Bucket Analogy (via speed expert Ken Clark): Have the athlete imagine they're holding three buckets–one balanced on top of their head, one atop their frontside thigh, and one hanging by the handle from their frontside toe. *Don't spill any of the 3 buckets*. This will demand a neutral head, thigh split, and dorsiflexed ankle–all critical elements in an efficient sprinting posture.

2. The head, hips, and backside heel should align.

3. Neutral pelvis: The bulk of our A-Series work will occur with the hands on the hips so that athletes receive tactile feedback as to whether or not their pelvis stays neutral throughout the movement. If pelvic positioning has not already been taught along with the basic movement patterns in Section 1, now is the time to teach it via pelvic tilts.

4. Vertical leg action: Some like to cue this like pistons. For those not as mechanically inclined, they can be cued to attack the ground *under* the hips. We do not want athletes reaching or "casting" their foot out in front of the body during speed work.

The A-Position (3 Bucket Position)

A-SERIES DRILLS

1. The A-March
    a. Stand tall with head, hip, heel alignment.
    b. Place the hands on the hips.
    c. Drive one leg into the A-Position (3 bucket position).
    d. Punch the ground under the hips as the legs switch.
    e. Continue marching through the A-Pattern.
    f. There will ALWAYS be one foot on the ground in this drill.
    g. The pattern is R-L-R-L.

PURPOSE	CUES	PRESCRIPTION
VERTICAL POSTURE	HEAD, HIP, HEEL	2x10-15 yds/m
NEUTRAL PELVIS	3 BUCKET POSITION	
PUSHING ACTION	PUNCH GROUND UNDER HIPS	

2. The A-Pop
   a. Stand tall with head, hip, heel alignment.
   b. Hands on hips.
   c. Raise one foot into a low A-Position (about mid-shin height).
   d. Pop the ground under the hips so that both feet temporarily float.
   e. Skip into the low A-Position on the opposite leg.
   f. The pattern is R-L-R-L.

PURPOSE	CUES	PRESCRIPTION
RHYTHM	POP, FLOAT, SKIP	2x15-20 yds/m
RELAXATION		
VERTICAL EMPHASIS		

3. The A-Skip
   a. Stand tall with head, hip, heel alignment.
   b. Skip into A-Position (3 buckets).
   c. The pattern is LL-RR-LL-RR.

PURPOSE	CUES	PRESCRIPTION
RHYTHM	PUSH OUT	2x15-20 yds/m
RELAXATION	PUNCH DOWN	
HORIZONTAL EMPHASIS		

4. The A-Switch
   a. Stand tall with head, hip, heel alignment.
   b. Begin in A-Position (3 buckets), on one leg.
   c. Quickly switch to the A-Position on the other leg, attacking the ground under the hips.
   d. Single A-Switch:
      i. Pattern is R-L-R-L-R-L
   e. Double A-Switch:
      i. Pattern is RL-RL-RL or LR-LR-LR
   f. Triple A-Switch:
      i. Pattern is RLR-LRL-RLR-LRL

PURPOSE	CUES	PRESCRIPTION
VERTICAL EMPHASIS	3 BUCKETS	2x10-15 yds/m
	PUNCH DOWN	

SPEED DEVELOPMENT METHODS – ACCELERATION AND MAXIMUM VELOCITY

Acceleration Work

Don't overthink this!

The methods are simple:

1. Cue the athlete to *start slow and finish fast*. While counterintuitive to not get out of the proverbial blocks as fast as possible, studies have shown that accelerating with the intent of gradually reaching top speed results in

higher peak speed in team sport athletes versus trying to accelerate maximally. This is likely due to how critical it is to be relaxed in order to reach top-end speed. As the military saying goes: *slow is smooth and smooth is fast.*

2. Autoregulate intensity by controlling distance. A 30-yard acceleration will induce more fatigue than a 10-yard acceleration. This is not only because of the greater distance, but because of the greater speed reached and greater input from the central nervous system (CNS) required to reach that speed.

3. Manage volume. The emphasis here is speed development, *not* conditioning. Volumes are as follows:

VOLUME PARAMETERS*
LOW = 100-150 yards/meters
MODERATE = 150-250 yards/meters
HIGH = 250-300 yards/meters

*Remember, you're going to need ~30-60 seconds of rest for every 10 yards sprinted. It is unlikely that you will ever have the time–or need to take the time–with a volleyball player to hit a high volume speed session. I generally live in the low volume range with my athletes, particularly since most are competing year round.

4. Vary the athlete's starting position. Volleyball isn't played exclusively out of a two-point stance. Though we've discussed at length why it's unnecessary to make everything specific to the sport, it is important to teach the body to accelerate out of multiple positions.
   a. Two-point stance – start with the feet staggered. If you really want to split hairs, the front shin angle should be approximately 60 degrees with the

torso angle similar. Remember, in acceleration we want to produce more horizontal force. Starting with a greater shin angle sets the athlete up to get "tall" earlier in the sprint than you want for optimal acceleration. More specific to the sport of volleyball, it is rarely a good thing to stand up when accelerating in defense. ASK ME HOW I KNOW.

b. Universal athletic position into plyo step – start in a ready position with the hips and feet square. Cue the athlete to sink, split the feet, and project off the line.

This will have the athlete complete what was commonly mislabeled as a "false step." For years, coaches have been on a witch hunt instructing athletes not to step back to go forward. However, if you watch elite athletes in ANY sport, you will see them do exactly this: split one foot back into a position to apply horizontal force. Efficient movement is about displacing the body's center of mass, not just the foot. A forward step is not only unnatural, it's also inefficient (which is why EVERY athlete plyo steps unless a coach ruins it). Why? Because a forward step displaces the foot only. The hips haven't moved. In fact, the foot out in front of the hip serves as a brake, forcing the athlete to drag their entire body across the front foot in order to cover any ground. If they aren't already too late from this atrocity, they will have to get their feet back into position to strike under the hip if they are to have any prayer of getting to the ball.

Conversely, an athlete that completes a plyo step has their feet in position to project the body *forward* (or laterally if that's the desired direction). It's very basic physics. I apply backwards force into the ground to project my body forward. Newton's 3rd Law for the readers like me who are/were science teachers.

c. Blind start – have the athletes lay on their stomach and get up and sprint. This is great for volleyball athletes, as they may have to dive to dig a ball and quickly get up to attack, block, or retreat to their defensive position.

All of these start positions can be varied to include forward, lateral, and backward variations.

5. Acceleration progressions:
    a. Hill sprints
    b. Resisted sprints

A sample acceleration focused training session is as follows:

EXERCISE	PARAMETERS
A-March	2x10 yds
A-Switch (single)	2x10 yds
A-Skip	2x15 yds
10 Yard Accelerations	x8-10 - multiple start positions
Total Volume = 80-100 yards	

Maximum Velocity Work

Just like with acceleration, keep this simple. Want your athletes to sprint fast? TIME THEM. Don't have timing gates and are trying to get 60 athletes through a speed session with 2 coaches and a pair of stopwatches? Turn it into a race.

For timed sprints, I like using flying 10s, where the final 10 yards/meters are timed, and there is a "fly-in" zone of 5-20 yards/meters. Remember, the longer the sprint the higher the speed, and the more fatiguing it will be on the athlete's central nervous system. With longer sprints, not only will greater recovery time be needed *within* the session, but then also *between* sessions.

Parameters are simple:

1. For team sport athletes, the primary focus will be distances of 20-30 yards or less.

2. Volume and recovery can mirror what was covered in the acceleration section of the chapter, at 30-60 seconds per 10 yards.

For untimed sprints, "rabbit runs" can increase intent during the training session. From a variety of starting positions, have athletes work in pairs or groups of similar speed. One athlete will serve as the "rabbit," the other the "hound." There are a few ways to structure this:

1. The rabbit initiates the drill off of their movement. When they take off, the other athletes react and pursue. In this case, I would start the rabbit about a half yard behind the hounds, since the rabbit has the advantage of knowing when the rep is going to start.

2. A second variant is to start the rabbit slightly in front of the rest of the group (depending on speed), and the coach initiates the start on a whistle or "go" command.

Regardless of how you structure the session, each rep should be performed at 95%+ effort with recovery times adjusted accordingly.

A sample maximal velocity session is as follows:

EXERCISE	PARAMETERS
A-March	2x10 yds
A-Switch (double)	2x10 yds
A-Pop	2x15 yds
20 yard Acceleration	1 rep up to 50%, 1x75%, 1x95%
Flying 10 yard sprint	x3 timed reps with 10 yard drop-in zone
Total Volume = 120 yards	

CHAPTER NINE:
PLYOMETRICS &
CHANGE OF DIRECTION

After 8 chapters, the wait is *finally* over. This is what you came for. The Holy Grail of volleyball: plyometrics. All hail the vertical jump!!!

But first let's pack a bag, we're going to the beach!! Humor me and write down a few items you might pack in your bag. I'll share mine:

- Towel
- Sunscreen
- Sunglasses
- Chair
- Water
- SNACKS

Your list is probably similar.

One item you don't see on my list that likely isn't on your list either? *Sand.* Why on Earth would we bring more sand to the beach when there's already plenty there? We wouldn't, because that's dumb.

Yet this is *exactly* what many do with their volleyball strength and conditioning programs. They ignore every other physical capacity and focus exclusively on the one training bucket that is already overflowing: plyometrics and jump training.

Conversely, I spend relatively little time on plyometrics and jump training in the athletic development of a volleyball player. I realize this approach is tipping the sacred cow of the sport, but we are no longer in an era where volleyball is played only a few months out of the year, and our training programs need to reflect that.

When including plyometrics and jumps in the training program, I do so with a purpose greater than *"I want the athletes to jump higher."* While one would be foolish to ignore the importance of the vertical jump for a volleyball player, there are a few additional factors at play. More on the purpose of jump training and plyometrics in a bit, but first let's quibble over semantics:

Jumps: Jumps are simple: you jump and you land. These will help you train the *skill* of jumping and the rate of force development (RFD).

Plyometrics: Plyometrics aren't quite as simple: you jump, land, and *immediately* jump again, sometimes multiple times in a series. These help train elasticity/reactivity, qualities that are critical when attempting to change directions or execute multiple jumps in a row.

One point of clarification is that plyometrics are not necessarily superior to jumping in every scenario (or vice versa), but each have advantages over the other in certain contexts. Knowing what each one trains can aid in understanding when they might be better put to use.

As mentioned previously, plyometrics are more than just jumping high. To further break down their function, we will be leaving behind our sunscreen and beach umbrella, placing all the snacks in my bag (for safekeeping of course), and plunging into the Arctic for a top-to-bottom view of the plyometric iceberg.

The Plyometric Iceberg

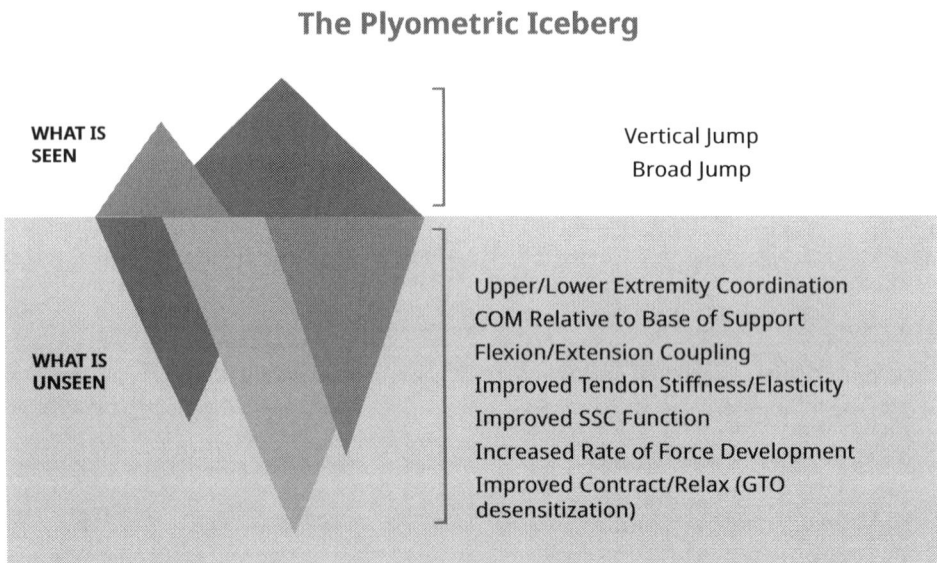

WHAT IS SEEN

Vertical Jump
Broad Jump

WHAT IS UNSEEN

Upper/Lower Extremity Coordination
COM Relative to Base of Support
Flexion/Extension Coupling
Improved Tendon Stiffness/Elasticity
Improved SSC Function
Increased Rate of Force Development
Improved Contract/Relax (GTO desensitization)

The portion of the plyometric iceberg that most see? The vertical jump and broad jump– which, as we just learned, aren't actually plyometrics at all.

162

But as you're likely aware, any good iceberg has an enormous volume of ice that lies beneath the water's surface. The above graphic shows the many relevant outcomes of a well-designed plyometric training program, most of which have to do with an athlete's ability to react quickly, a critical skill in the sport of volleyball.

Still not convinced?

Wearable technology is starting to paint a pretty clear picture that maximum height jumping only represents about 40% of the volleyball equation. The Stanford Women's Volleyball team conducted a two year study during which they looked at the heights of every jump that occurred in training, practice, and competition.

The table below shows a breakdown of the number of jumps within each height category:

JUMP HEIGHTS BY CATEGORY		
Jump Class	n	Percent
Band 1 (<6in)	1530	0.93
Band 2 (7-15in)	98211	59.59
Band 3 (>15in)	65072	39.48

As you can see, only 40% of these jumps were greater than 15 inches! (And I'm sure you're already aware that 15 inches isn't an impressive vertical for a Division I Women's Volleyball Player.)

So what does this data mean? While max height jumping has clear relevance to the sport of volleyball, your athletes need exposure to more than just max height jumping/plyometrics in training. They need to train a variety of different types of plyometrics and jumps in order to prepare their tissues for what they will encounter in the sport.

PLYOMETRIC CATEGORIES

Plyometrics are generally broken down into two broad categories: extensive and intensive. The tables below go into more depth on each of the two categories, but in general:

Extensive Plyometrics = Lower height and faster ground contact times (GCT). These are less stressful on the athlete and will make up about 80% of the training volume I prescribe during the week.

Intensive Plyometrics = Higher height and longer GCTs. Intensive plyos are more stressful on the athlete and will make up only about 20% of the training volume I prescribe throughout the week.

EXTENSIVE PLYOMETRICS			
PROPERTIES	**BENEFITS**	**EXAMPLES**	**PARAMETERS**
Low amplitude	Train stiffness/reactivity	Pogo hops (in place)	80% of weekly plyo volume
Lower ground reaction forces (GRF)	Build tissue tolerance	Skater Hops	Emphasize FAST GCT
Fast ground contact time (GCT)	Develop coordination	Low hurdle hops (~less than 12")	Total Weekly Volume: 80-200 Contacts

INTENSIVE PLYOMETRICS			
PROPERTIES	**BENEFITS**	**EXAMPLES**	**PARAMETERS**
High amplitude (max effort)	Train landing mechanics from max height jump	Broad jump into vertical jump	20% of weekly plyo volume
High GRF	High CNS activation	Drop jump	Emphasize max intent
Higher GCT	Improve vertical jump	Lateral hurdle hop to box jump	Total Weekly Volume: 20-50 contacts

PROGRESSING PLYOMETRICS

Some coaches progress plyometrics in a linear fashion, beginning exclusively with extensive plyometrics before progressing to jumps and intensive plyometrics. With my athletes, however, I include some maximal intent or near maximal intent *jumping* throughout the training process. The way I see it, the athlete is already doing this in the sport as it is, so it's a mistake to not prepare them to land properly from higher amplitude jumps. As such, my progression is as follows:

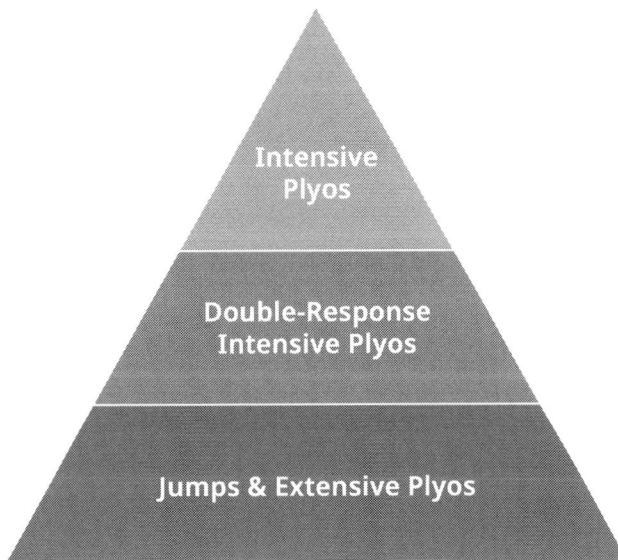

We begin with extensive plyos and jumps and then progress into double-response intensive plyos. These are plyos where, instead of going immediately into the next jump, the athlete lands and completes a "bounce" in place to gather themselves before transitioning into the next rep.

This is an enormously helpful transition into intensive plyometrics for developmental athletes. Plyometrics as a whole are predicated on having a short ground contact time; and, as the name implies, intensive plyos are *intense*. It takes a lot of reactive strength to execute these plyometrics, which many athletes will lack at this stage. Consequently, they will default to a long ground contact time in an attempt to gather themselves for a second big effort. The result? The exercise in question is no longer a plyometric, it's a jump. Again, this is completely fine if our aim is, in fact, just to jump. But if we are seeking the additional benefits of plyometrics, a faster ground contact time is essential. The double-response plyo solves this issue. It allows athletes to shorten their ground contact time because the "bounce" is really just an extensive plyometric that they can easily complete at their current level of strength prior to their second big output.

An example would be:

High hurdle jump > land & immediately bounce > land & jump over second hurdle

From there, the program will progress to intensive plyos.

But not all extensive and intensive plyometrics are equal. Within each category, we will progress from:

Bilateral to unilateral landings, aka double-leg to single-leg

AND

Single-plane to multi-planar jumps and plyos

An example of a single-plane plyometric would be a continuous skater jump (frontal plane). To make that multi-planar, we might complete a skater jump (frontal plane) then hop forward onto a 4-6 inch box (sagittal plane).

PLYOMETRIC VOLUME

Where it comes to volume, a known industry standard comes from the National Strength and Conditioning Association. Their guidelines for plyometric volume by session are as follows:

- **Beginner** (no experience) = 80-100 contacts per session
- **Intermediate** (some experience) = 100-120 contacts per session
- **Advanced** (considerable experience) = 120-140 contacts per session

The recommendations listed in the tables above account for two jump/plyometric sessions per week and I generally err on the low end of the NSCA's recommendations. Additionally, when calculating volume I place jumps in the intensive plyometric category. While they don't include the same level of central nervous system input that intensive plyometrics have, they tend to be completed with maximal intent, which requires athletes to dissipate large amounts of force during jump landings. As such, jumps can be fairly stressful on an athlete's joints and soft tissue.

A sample plyometric session for beginners is as follows:

EXERCISE	PARAMETERS
Pogo Hops	2x15
12" Hurdle Hops – Forward	3x5 hurdles – stick & hold each landing
Skater Hop	2x5e – stick & hold each landing
Jump to Box	2x5 – stick & hold each landing
Total Volume = 75 Contacts (65 Extensive/10 Intensive)	

THE UNIVERSAL ATHLETIC POSITION

The foundation of teaching jumps, plyometrics, and change of direction is the Universal Athletic Position (UAP). Training this movement is essential in every sport, but many overlook it due to its simplicity. It could easily have been an earlier chapter of this book; however, in an attempt to trick you into not skipping over it, I've included it here in the Holy Grail chapter on plyometrics.

The reason the UAP is so vital to the sport of volleyball is that it directly relates to teaching proper landing and cutting mechanics, both of which are critical in the reduction of risk to the ACL and other soft tissues. The deceleration phase of landing and/or cutting is when non-contact soft tissue injuries often occur, so it is essential that we ingrain this position early in an athlete's career. Not only is it important from an injury reduction standpoint, the UAP is also valuable from a movement proficiency standpoint. Much of the UAP's benefit lies in teaching an athlete how to keep their center of mass within their base of support. Athletes who cannot own this position in training will not find it when the game is on the line, when all of a sudden they must quickly change directions to get to a pass, set, or block.

UAP BASICS

1.   Place the feet shoulder distance apart with the toes pointed forward.

2.   Bend the knees and reach the hips back so that the weight is distributed across the midfoot. (Do not coach "being on your toes." This is an awful position for balance and force application. In fact, I tell athletes I should barely be able to see their heels off the ground.)

3.   The spine should be neutral and the chest should be out.

4.   The shoulders should be over the balls of the feet so that the torso angle and shin angle are similar.

5.   The arms should be bent to 90 degrees with the elbows slightly behind the shoulders. If you want to modify this to whatever your preferred arm position is for volleyball? Knock yourself out.

6.   The eyes should be forward.

UNIVERSAL ATHLETIC POSITION PROGRESSION 1: ISOMETRIC HOLDS

Very simple: line your players up and have them hold the position for time. This allows a quick scan of the room while walking around and giving feedback to athletes on their position. Additionally, you can spot-check who is and who isn't balanced by lightly pushing the athletes' shoulders. An athlete sitting back into their heels? They'll usually step back with even a little bit of contact. Those who aren't braced at the spine? They'll sway with contact.

The UAP (Universal Athletic Position)

Begin with a 15-20 second hold and progress to around 30 seconds.

UAP PROGRESSION 3: STEPS ON THE WHISTLE

Next, we begin incorporating movements that begin and end in the UAP. We also want to train *staying* in the UAP throughout the movement, because that's kind of important in sports.

1. Start all athletes in a UAP iso hold.

2. Cue them to step either:
    a. Left (resetting immediately into UAP).

  b. Right (resetting immediately into UAP).

  c. Forward into a split stance (holding this split position before resetting).

  d. Backward into a split stance (holding this split position before resetting).

3. Perform 2-3 sets lasting approximately 30 seconds. Not only are we teaching proper movement from the UAP, we are also building strength and endurance in this critical position.

Split Stance UAP

UAP PROGRESSION 3 (PLYOS/JUMPS): JUMPS TO A BOX

As alluded to previously, the number one priority early in a jump training or plyometric program should be teaching athletes how to safely land, effectively dissipating force through the tissues intended to receive those forces. Athletes of low training age will frequently attempt to land/cut with limited knee and hip flexion, leading to a much higher risk of an ACL rupture along with an increased risk in developing overuse injuries like patellar tendonitis or "jumper's knee." Teaching them to land in the UAP with the proper degree of knee and hip flexion leads to greater loading at the hip, and a reduced risk of injury. Jumps to a box can be a great way to accomplish this, and one that athletes enjoy.

But use caution. While landing with *limited* knee flexion and hip flexion isn't safe or athletic, landing with *excessive* hip and knee flexion (and often a rounded spine) isn't either. It also is *not* indicative of jumping higher. Instead, this is indicative of an improperly selected box height.

Please read this very carefully: *jump height is determined by vertical displacement of the athlete's center of mass, not by the height of the box.*

While a higher box can, at times, drive intent, it is inappropriate to sacrifice landing mechanics for height, particularly early in an athlete's development. This practice is *all risk, no reward* since the athlete isn't jumping any higher or prepared to make any maneuver after landing, which is generally required by the sport of volleyball. They are simply tucking the knees to the chest in order to get their feet onto the box.

Speaking of boxes, with that out of the way I'll climb down off that soapbox and get to the point. Here are the steps to teaching the jump to a box:

1. Select a box height for each athlete that allows them to land in UAP.

2. Jump off of two feet and land onto the box in UAP.

3. Cue jumping *onto* the height of the box, not *to* the height of the box, so the athlete uses maximal intent.

4. Hold the UAP for 2-3 seconds.

5. Step off the box (do not jump off the box) and repeat.

Landing On Box in UAP

Common errors:

1. Loud landings. Cue the athlete to land softly or quietly.

2. Continuing to sink at the hips upon landing. While this will sound like it's in direct opposition to "landing soft," they need to hit the landing like a brick–meaning, they are braced to stop on impact.

3. Valgus movement at the knees (aka the knees caving in). Cue the athlete to rip the floor apart upon landing, just as we cued during the squat. You can also place a band around the athlete's knees to provide an external cue to eliminate valgus movement upon landing. Eliminate the box or reduce the box height when placing a band around the athlete's knees.

Progressions:

1. Jump off of two feet, land on one foot.

2. Lateral jump to box.

3. 90 degree turn-jump to box. Start with the box to the athlete's left. Jump, turning 90 degrees in the air and landing in UAP on the box.

UAP PROGRESSION 4 (PLYOS/JUMPS): BOX STEP-OFFS

Because the athlete is required to dissipate more force in this movement than in a jump to the box, I don't start my teaching progression with box step-offs.

1. Begin with an athlete standing on an 8-18" box, bench, or bleacher.

2. *Step* off of the box.

3. Land in the UAP and hold for 2-3 seconds.

Common Errors:

1. Two separate foot contacts versus landing simultaneously on both feet. Cue them to hear one contact.

2. Loud landings–see above.

3. Continuing to sink into landing–see above.

4. Valgus movement at the knee–see above.

Progressions:

1. Increase the height of the box.*

2. Step off of the box, stick and hold landing on one foot.

3. Drop jumps (no arms): with hands on hips, step off the box, land, and immediately jump again. Stick and hold the second landing.

4. Step off into acceleration. Step off of the box, land in UAP. Plyo step into a 5-10 yard acceleration.

*A few notes on box height as it pertains to box step-offs:

1. It is unlikely your athletes will require "altitude drops," where they land from heights greater than their vertical jump at this developmental stage in their career. For what it's worth, I didn't use altitude drops with Division I volleyball players either.

2. In my opinion, depth jumps (where the athlete lands from a height greater than their vertical jump and immediately takes off into a second jump) are wholly unnecessary to see improvement at this stage in their career. Another training tool I didn't subject my Division I volleyball players to and yet we all lived to tell the story.

As discussed in Chapter 1, *both* of these movements present potentially higher risk than is necessary given that tremendous improvements in athleticism can be made without their use. Don't do it for likes on social media or because you saw an elite level athlete do it. *Do it for the athlete in front of you and what's best for their development.*

With that being the case, I generally stop at an 18-inch box and on rare occasions use up to 24-inches. A truth that will be unpopular with depth jump enthusiasts: an 18-inch box is going to be effective enough for most high school athletes and many collegiate athletes as well.

UAP PROGRESSION 4A (CHANGE OF DIRECTION): 5-0-5 WITH PAUSES

Though disappointing for some, this book will not cover agility in great detail. The reality is that what many consider agility (ladders, running around cones, 5-0-5 and 5-10-5 drills) is not agility, it's change of direction (COD). In the case of ladders, they're a nice tool for working general coordination with very young athletes or warming up older ones, but are generally quite a poor tool for teaching athletes how to efficiently move in and out of cuts.

Agility training requires reacting to an actual stimulus, and even the best mirror drills do not train the cognitive-perceptual elements required to react to the ball on the volleyball court. I could also make the case that if in a game I see my players executing an overabundance of agility maneuvers at the types of distances cone drills usually cover...then as a coach what I really need to do is take a hard look at:

- Blocking schemes
- Passing percentages
- Defensive reads

But that's probably a different book.

Yes, I know things get out of system and sometimes these are the long, wild rallies that impact the game heavily by...scoring a single point. But, regardless, I would prefer to train agility in practice through the types of small-sided games that actually impact a player's ability to perceive the game at game speeds.

Nonetheless, we do want to spend *some* time working on efficient COD using the UAP, which I'll train using a regressed version of the 5-0-5 drill.

1. Start facing a line 5 yards in front of the athlete (in the volleyball gym, start on the serving line with the 10-foot line as your destination).

2. Sprint towards the line.

3. Come to a stop on the line in a split stance UAP. The athlete should be balanced. Hold this position for 2-3 seconds, finding balance if not already there.

4. Backpedal back to the start line again coming to a stop in a split stance UAP.

Hold this position for 2-3 seconds, finding balance if not already there.

Though I pride myself on attention to detail, this is not where I split hairs over touching lines. If an athlete stops short of the line or slightly past the line because that's where their stride naturally took them? Cool. We're here to work on the position they are decelerating in, not on touching lines.

To address multiple planes of motion, we use different patterns in this 5-0-5 drill:

1. Lateral shuffle - Pause in UAP - Lateral shuffle - Pause in UAP

2. Sprint - Pause in split stance UAP - Open & Lateral shuffle (Left) - Pause in UAP

3. Sprint - Pause in split stance UAP - Open & Lateral shuffle (Right) - Pause in UAP

4. Lateral shuffle - Pause in UAP - Open and Sprint - Pause in split stance UAP

Progression:

1. Extend the distance out to 10 yards. The increased entry speed will increase the deceleration demands.

UAP PROGRESSION 4B (CHANGE OF DIRECTION): 5-0-5 WITHOUT PAUSES

1. This is exactly the same as above, but removing pauses so the athlete is cutting at the greatest speed attainable at the prescribed distance of either 5 or 10 yards.

Common errors in COD work:

1. The center of mass is too high. Cue athletes to come into cuts low.

2. The shoulders or center of mass (COM) get outside of the base of support. Often, this comes from athletes "reaching" to get to a cut and trying to avoid this is the reason I don't fixate on whether or not athletes touch the line during the teaching progressions for COD work. Cue athletes to always have one foot under their COM.

3. A negative shin angle. Generally, if we clean up errors 1&2, it will autocorrect the shin angle.

An efficient way to get a large number of athletes through COD drills is with the use of "the grid." The grid method may not have been invented by my friend Kyle Keese at Denton Guyer High School, but he is widely known for promoting its use and therefore gets credit for it in this book.

A grid setup is as follows, with three different athletes represented by three different arrow types:

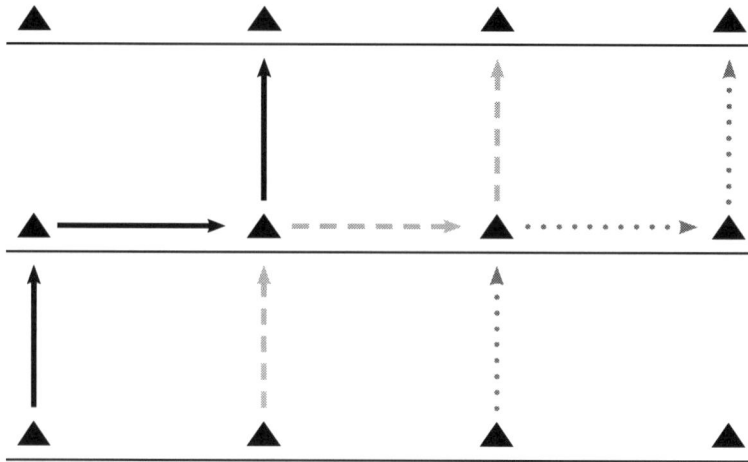

In this example an athlete might sprint ahead to the first cone, shuffle laterally to the cone to their right, then sprint to the next cone directly ahead of them. This can be easily manipulated to include pauses at each cone in the early stages and higher speed changes of direction in later phases. It can also be manipulated to include multiple movement patterns:

- Sprint
- Backpedal
- Crossover run
- Shuffle
- Gallop

And can be manipulated to include multiple angles of cuts:

- 45 degrees
- 90 degrees
- 135 degrees
- 180 degrees

There is no secret to the grid, it is just a simple way to organize a COD session and get a lot of kids moving at the same time.

VOLUME FOR CHANGE OF DIRECTION OR AGILITY WORK

VOLUME BY SESSION
LOW = 60-100 yards/meters
MODERATE = 100-150 yards/meters
HIGH = 150-200 yards/meters

Due to time constraints–along with the high volume of COD/agility work that will be organically incorporated into practice and competition–I tend to program sessions on the low volume end of the spectrum and have still had good success.

A sample COD session for a beginner athlete might look as follows:

EXERCISE	PARAMETERS
UAP Iso Hold	2x20 seconds
UAP Steps on Whistle	2x6-8 steps
The Grid with Pauses	4x20 yards (varied patterns in 5 yard segments)
Total Volume = 80 yards	

CHAPTER TEN:
CONDITIONING

For some, this chapter may create cognitive dissonance as it goes against the cherished belief that one must "outwork" opponents in order to be successful. To help dial that back a bit, before reading any further, please revisit the Youth Physical Development Models (Figures 2 and 3) in Chapter 1 with the following question in mind:

Where does metabolic conditioning fall in the realm of importance for youth and adolescent athletes?

As you can tell by looking at the figures, and having answered this same question at the start of Section 2, priority-wise, metabolic conditioning falls well below the capacities of strength, hypertrophy, speed, power, and agility.

Despite this truth, there are still entire off-season programs that are almost exclusively devoted to conditioning. Worse, they're devoted to *poorly-designed conditioning*, for the express purpose of making athletes tired so the coaches "feel" the session was productive.

Creating fatigue for the purpose of creating fatigue should *never* be the goal of training. Remember: *performance is more important than hard work.*

This truth may make sense from a physiological standpoint, but still leave traditionalists to wonder:

What happens to mental toughness if we deemphasize conditioning?

I'm so glad you asked!

Nothing. Nothing at all. Because mental and physical toughness, while often conflated, are not the same thing.

I can run athletes until they puke, but it is highly unlikely that this style of training will keep an athlete from choking when the game is on the line. The mental toughness to execute under pressure comes from having faced similar pressures in practice or previous competitions and having both the desire and confidence to execute the required skill when the situation demands it. No athlete has time to "think about all the running we did during the off-season" when the opposing attacker detonates on a ball and they *have to* dig it or lose the game. These workouts might raise the stakes, but a team that needs to be motivated to win by an off-season running program will likely not be that successful because they clearly aren't motivated by the self-reinforcing behavior of winning.

So if toughness isn't the goal of our conditioning program, what is?

The goal of any well-designed conditioning program is to develop the physiological systems that make speed, power, and strength outputs *repeatable*.

To use slightly more scientific terminology: volleyball requires a tremendous number of anaerobic efforts, which are made more repeatable by a well-developed aerobic energy system. Numerous conditioning "gurus" have emerged over the years, promoting the idea that the aerobic energy system can be developed by using anaerobic training. There's some truth to this notion, but its implementation typically comes at a higher metabolic and mechanical cost than lower-intensity aerobic sessions–a price athletes often cannot afford due to the overall demands of training and competition.

However, despite there being value to lower intensity conditioning, the LAST thing I want volleyball athletes doing is participating in a long-distance running program! There is nothing about long-distance running that will benefit a volleyball player.

Long, slow, distance running won't make them faster. It won't make them jump higher. Instead, done often enough, it will make them slower and decrease their vertical. It may also lead to lower limb injury, since this area is already placed under tremendous load by the sport.

Fortunately, there's a way to develop an athlete's aerobic energy system that doesn't come at the higher cost of anaerobic training or carry the potential to decrease speed/power/strength outputs like long-distance running.

Enter the cardiac output circuit.

CARDIAC OUTPUT CIRCUITS

1. Choose 5 exercises from the following menu of exercises (or use your own):

FUNDAMENTAL MOVEMENT SKILLS	EXTENSIVE MED BALL THROWS	LOADED MOVEMENTS
Leopard Crawl	Medicine Ball Slam	Farmer's Carry (50-75% BW)
10 Yard Shuffle	Medicine Ball Rainbow Slam	Bwd Sled Drag (50-75% BW)
Forward/Backward Run	Bwd Overhead Throw + Chase	Lateral Sled Drag (40-50% BW)

2. Use one of the following methods to determine intensity:
    a. Heart Rate: 65-75% of an athlete's max heart rate.
    b. Rate of Perceived Exertion: 6-7 RPE (on a 10 point scale).
    c. *Unforced* nasal breathing–breathing exclusively through the nose both during inhalation and exhalation. If an athlete needs to gasp for air through their mouth, the intensity is too high. Efforts should be scaled back until they can breathe comfortably again using only their nose.

For most, unforced nasal breathing will be the most practical solution for large groups of athletes and will autoregulate the intensity of the session.

3. Perform the first selected exercise for 30 seconds. Rest for 30 seconds. Complete the second exercise with a work:rest of 30:30. Repeat until you've completed all 5 exercises (5 total minutes).

4.   Rest for 1 minute.

5.   Repeat for 3-5 sets for a total of 18-30 minutes.

6.   Complete these circuits 1-2 times a week.

A sample cardiac output circuit is as follows:

MOVEMENT	WORK INTERVAL	REST INTERVAL
10 Yard Shuffle	:30	:30
Medicine Ball Slam	:30	:30
Lateral Sled Drag	:30	:30
Farmer's Carry	:30	:30
Leopard Crawl	:30	:30
Rest between sets: 1-minute **Complete 3-5 sets**		

These cardiac output circuits check a lot of boxes:

1.   Provides athletes with a stimulus to develop the aerobic energy system without inducing unnecessary fatigue.

2.   Provides an effective method for active recovery. I use these on Mondays with athletes who had a tournament the prior weekend. The cardiac output circuit replaces the regularly scheduled speed/strength session they may not be recovered enough to benefit from.

3.   If you're the strength coach...it can be challenging to convince your pesky sport coach that training doesn't need to be full-send all the time. With so much movement occurring during these circuits, sport coaches believe

athletes are working harder than they are. When educating a sport coach fails, stealth is critical.

4. Athletes leave the session feeling better than when they started.

SECTION 3:
REDUCING THE LIKELIHOOD OF COMMON VOLLEYBALL INJURIES

Scan the QR Code to watch the Demo Videos that correspond with the Exercise Progressions and Images listed in Section 3:

This section will focus on the commonly injured areas of the:

- Shoulder
- Knee
- Low Back

However, it is important to understand that injury reduction isn't a separate program that we prescribe. *It is the program.* While this chapter will discuss a few targeted exercises to address common injuries, 90% of injury reduction will come as a result of implementing the principles and methods outlined in the surrounding chapters. This chapter is the icing on the cake, not the cake itself. Sitting around eating spoonfuls of icing by itself is gross. Really gross, and yet somehow a lot less gross than pretending a Thera-Band tied to the net is going to save weak athletes with poor movement patterns from a shoulder injury.

It is also important to understand that not all injuries can be prevented. As mentioned in Chapter 1, genetics matter. The training (or lack thereof) that occurred before the athlete was in your program matters. The other 23 hours in an athlete's day matter. When it comes to injury reduction, nearly everything matters.

We can't *prevent* all injuries. The best we can do is everything in our power to reduce the likelihood that they occur.

CHAPTER ELEVEN:
INJURY REDUCTION OF THE SHOULDER, KNEE, AND LOW BACK

An important framework for understanding injury to any given joint is Mike Boyle's "Joint By Joint Approach to Training." The basic premise is that the joints of the body alternate with a greater need for stability and a greater need for mobility.

Foot - greater need for stability

Ankle - greater need for mobility

Knee - stability

Hip - mobility

Lumbar spine - stability

Thoracic spine - mobility

Scapula - stability

Shoulder - mobility

Elbow - stability

Wrist - mobility

If the function of a given joint is compromised, it will likely create issues in the joints above or below it. As an example, an athlete with restricted ankle mobility is potentially at a higher risk for an ACL tear or other knee issues. Why? Because the human body is an outstanding cheater. If the ankle is unable to do its job, but the sporting movement demands that a movement occurs, the knee will step in and try to fill that role. If the knee, which is really only intended to perform one function (flexion/extension), is loaded beyond what it can bear...KAPOW goes the ACL, MCL, or meniscus. You can observe similar occurrences in other joints.

Given this concept, it should immediately become obvious that strategies to reduce injury in one joint will require a holistic approach, versus an isolated focus on the joint in question. As I've mentioned several times throughout this book: attempting to reduce the likelihood of injuring a specific joint isn't a separate training program, *it is the training program.*

Nonetheless, what follows are a few considerations for each of the common injuries in the sport of volleyball.

THE SHOULDER

Given what was just discussed regarding the joint-by-joint approach, it should come as no surprise that the function of the scapula is critical to shoulder health. In order for the arm to achieve a full overhead range of motion, the athlete's shoulder blade must be able to upwardly rotate and posteriorly tilt.

To understand why, let's back up a bit. On the scapula, there is a bony process called the acromion. Beneath it, within the glenohumeral (shoulder) joint is what's known as the subacromial space. This is where the rotator cuff and bursa reside.

Upwardly rotating and posteriorly tilting the scapula opens up the subacromial space by getting the acromion process out of the way so that the arm can get overhead fully without compensation. If either of these two movements are compromised, the subacromial space is insufficient for unimpeded overhead movement. This eventually can lead to irritation, impingement, or fraying of the rotator cuff. A death sentence to an outside hitter's career.

The muscles responsible for these two movements are as follows:

MOVEMENT	MUSCLES
Scapular Upward Rotation	Serratus Anterior, Lower Trapezius, Upper Trap
Scapular Posterior Tilt	Serratus Anterior, Lower Trapezius

TRAINING THE SERRATUS ANTERIOR

To train the serratus anterior, first refer back to Chapter 5 – The Push-Up. One reason I am so adamant about proper push-up technique is that it has benefits well beyond what most eyes can see. By completing the movement through a full range of motion and actively pushing the chest away from the floor at the completion of the rep, we not only engage the triceps, we also engage the all-important serratus anterior.

In addition to push-ups, I program crawling patterns frequently to engage the serratus and promote scapular stability.

Leopard Crawls:

1. Begin with the athlete in a quadruped position (all fours). The spine should be neutral so that the eyes are looking slightly ahead of the hands and the low back is not arched.

2. Lift the knees off the floor so the athlete is in a four point stance with the hips in line with the shoulders.

3. Crawl using opposite arm-opposite leg motion, trying to keep the hips and shoulders level. For an outstanding external cue, place one of the athlete's shoes or a cone on their low back and tell them not to let it fall off as they move. This coaches a braced core without you having to say a word.

4. Varying patterns:
   a. Forward
   b. Backward
   c. Lateral
   d. "Spelling Bee" – have athletes crawl in the shape of letters to spell their name, team mascot, or slogan. This is excellent for small spaces.

Leopard Crawl (Setup)

Generally, I program crawling as part of a dynamic warm-up or as a superset between lower body weight room exercises. In either case, I program 2-3 sets of 10-15 yards; or in the case of the spelling bee, one word (6-8 letters) equals one set.

TRAINING THE LOWER TRAPEZIUS

The trapezius muscle has three regions: upper, middle, and lower. Each play a role in the mobility, stability, and overall health of the shoulder, with the lower trap serving to assist in:

- Scapular upward rotation
- Scapular depression
- Scapular posterior tilt
- Scapular retraction

Despite assisting in four critical functions of the shoulder–and its poor function often being associated with shoulder injuries–the lower trap is often overlooked in training. Let's remedy this by adding a few targeted exercises to our training program.

The Prone Y:

1. Lay face down on the floor or a bench.

2. Extend the arms overhead so that the body forms the letter "Y." The optimal angle is 135 degrees of abduction. The thumbs should be up toward the ceiling. It can be helpful to first have athletes stand up and put their arms at these angles while looking at you, modeling the position. Hopefully this will reduce the number of Y/T hybrids that would otherwise be observed.

3. From the prone position, brace the core and contract the glutes so the ribs don't flare during the movement.

4. The head should remain neutral, with the eyes toward the floor.

5. Cue the athlete to drive the bottom tip of the scapula towards the front of their body to posteriorly tilt the scap. An alternative is to "screw" the bottom tip of the scapula into the ribcage.

6. Lift the arms off the floor under control.

7. Lower back to start and repeat or hold the position for time.

8. Variation:

    a. Incline bench Y

Prone Y (Setup)

Prone Y (Finish)

Incline Bench Y (Setup)

Incline Bench Y (Finish)

ADDITIONAL ISOLATED SCAPULAR STABILITY MOVEMENTS

As discussed in Chapter 6 – Upper Body Pulling, retraction is an important function of the scapula as it relates to shoulder health. The following two exercises train this movement.

The Prone T:

1. Lay down on a floor or a bench.

2. Extend the arms out to the side so the hands are in line with the shoulders and the body forms the letter "T" with the palms forward and thumbs up.

3. Brace the core, contract the glutes, and ensure the head is neutral.

4. Lift the arms by retracting the shoulder blades.

5. Variation:
   a. Incline Bench T

6. Muscles trained: middle trapezius.

Prone T (Setup)

Prone T (Finish)

Incline Bench T (Setup)

Incline Bench T (Finish)

The Incline Cobra:

1. Lie face down on an incline bench (~45 degrees).

2. Begin with the arms hanging straight down under the shoulders, the palms facing back and the thumbs in, as if you were going to place a dollar in your front pocket.

3. Move the arms around the body until they are flush with the hips. The arms should have rotated so that the palms are now forward and the thumbs out as if you were going to move that dollar to your back pocket*.

4. Retract and depress the shoulder blades.

5. Muscles trained: middle trapezius, lower trapezius

Incline Bench Cobra (Setup)

Incline Bench Cobra (Finish)

*The dollar from the front pocket to the back pocket is a double-edged sword. On the one hand, it aids athletes in understanding that their shoulders should rotate during the movement. On the other hand, you'll have athletes try to wrap their arms too far behind their body to put the imaginary dollar in their imaginary back pocket. Simply explaining where the arms will finish should eliminate this issue. Again, a useful tip is to have the athletes run through these positions while standing.

All three of these exercises will be programmed in sets of 10-15 reps.

THE THORACIC SPINE

The thoracic spine is going to serve as our segue between the shoulder and the low back, with direct implications on the health of each. Since the scapula sits on the thoracic spine, the ability of the scapula to posteriorly tilt is directly related to the thoracic spine's ability to extend.

You've already snuck some thoracic extension into the training program by including the front squat, which directly loads this movement, along with cueing proper posture in literally every other movement. Given the large volume of thoracic extension work already included thus far, I'll only cover one exercise isolating thoracic extension.

Prone Thoracic Extension:

1. Lie on the stomach on the floor or bench with the arms overhead so that the elbows are bent and in line with the ears.

2. Place the palms flat on the floor inside of the elbows.

3. Ensure that the head is neutral, with the eyes down.

4. Begin by lightly pressing the elbows and palms into the floor. The athlete should *immediately* feel the thoracic extensors turn on.

5. Slowly lift the head and chest until only the ribs remain on the floor. This will not be a large range of motion. Ensure that the head stays in line with the spine throughout the movement.

6. Complete 5-8 reps.

Prone Thoracic Extension (Setup)

Prone Thoracic Extension (Finish)

In addition to the ability to extend, the thoracic spine needs to be able to rotate. Not only is this critical for generating power when serving and attacking, this rotation also heavily influences the health of an athlete's lumbar spine, an area very often injured in volleyball players.

The thoracic spine has 12 vertebrae, each with between about 3 and 4 degrees of rotation for a total of up to 45 degrees of rotation. The lumbar spine, on the other hand, has 5 vertebrae with about 1-3 degrees of rotation each, for a total of up to 15 degrees of rotation.

This should clearly demonstrate that the lumbar spine was not designed to produce or sustain large amounts of rotation. Unfortunately, as explained in the joint-by-joint model, if the thoracic spine is compromised and a movement needs to occur, the body will compensate by rotating through the lumbar spine. This can lead to issues at the facet joints, pars stress fractures, and/or spondylolisthesis. This is not a path we want to travel.

Instead, in addition to learning to brace at the lumbar spine (which we will cover in the next section), we also want to improve thoracic rotation.

Thoracic Rotation: The Upper Body Clamshell

1. Lie on the right side with the hips, knees, and ankles all at 90 degrees.

2. Squeeze an object between the knees. A foam roller or rolled-up towel works great for this.

3. Extend the arms out in front of the shoulders with the palms together.

4. Inhale and begin to open and rotate the shoulders, moving the left arm towards the ground behind their back, continuing until the athlete can no longer achieve a greater range of motion without losing pressure on the object between their knees. (The ideal position is the back side of their left shoulder flat on the floor.)

5. The eyes should follow the left fingertips so that the head turns.

6. Reach the arms wide and hold this position for 2-3 seconds.

7. Exhale and return to the starting position with the palms together.

8. Complete 5 reps on this side, then switch to the other side.

Upper Body Clamshell (Setup)

Upper Body Clamshell (Finish)

THE LUMBAR SPINE

At this point, this book has covered two key principles needed to successfully train the lumbar spine for stability:

1. Posterior pelvic tilt, with bracing to keep the spine neutral during movements.

2. Thoracic spine mobility to eliminate compensating using the lumbar spine.

The final installment, which will be included in an upcoming section, will be:

- Hip mobility

Since we've already considered a few strategies to protect the lumbar spine in previous sections, let's discuss what *not* to do to promote stability in the lumbar spine: traditional core training. This includes:

- Crunches
- Sit-ups
- Russian twists
- Side bends

Not only do these present an injury risk due to repeat flexion, extension, and rotation to an area of the body that is not designed to sustain this type of work, they also confer little benefit from a performance standpoint. The core should be a stable base on which to generate and transmit force–as such, athletes need to be taught to *resist* movement at the lumbar spine, not to *create* it.

Given the fact that volleyball often demands power production when the feet are no longer in contact with the ground, core stability is absolutely critical. By ignoring this principle and clinging to antiquated methodologies incorporating high volumes of "abs" at the end of a training session, we create an energy leak that causes athletes to lose power when serving, attacking, and blocking.

Further, volleyball players also lose the ability to accelerate and decelerate as effectively if they are unable to keep their center of mass within their base of support when landing or changing directions. Without getting too far down a rabbit hole, the inability to stabilize the torso is the unsung villain in the story of many ACL injuries, with the lower body attempting to compensate for poor movement patterns higher up the chain.

To recap, don't waste valuable training time with traditional core work. Focus instead on things that will positively impact performance: movements that teach athletes to resist flexion, extension, and rotation. The foundation of this will be plank variations.

THE FRONT PLANK

The position for this will be exactly as described for the high plank exercise in Chapter 5's push-up progression, but with the athlete on their forearms versus the hands.

1. The body should be in a straight line from head to heels.

2. The pelvis should be posteriorly tilted with the quads and glutes contracted and the core braced. I cue athletes to try to take the wrinkles out of the back of their shirt. From a bracing perspective, this means creating intra-abdominal pressure, *not* sucking their belly button to their spine.

3. The head should be neutral, with the chin pulled toward the back of the neck and the eyes between the wrists or hands.

4. The shoulders should be directly above the elbows.

5. Hold this position for time with as little movement as possible.

6. Most can begin with 20-30 seconds and progress up to 60 seconds. At the point that they are able to hold for 60 seconds I will reduce the time to 30 seconds and begin

adding load by placing a plate on the athlete's low back/hips. In the rare case that athletes are unable to hold a front plank for a short period of time, the movement can be regressed by having the athlete support themselves on their knees.

Front Plank

THE SIDE PLANK

The position will be similar to what was described in the front plank, with the body in a straight line from head to heels, but with the athlete supported on one arm.

1. The shoulder of the supporting arm should be directly above the elbow.

2. The top arm should be placed on the top hip, with the shoulders pulled back and down away from the ears.

3. The chin should be pulled back so that the chin is neutral and the head should be in line with the midline of the body. Do not allow the head to sag toward the ground.

4. The shoulders, hips, and heels should be in a straight line.

5. The feet should be stacked on top of one another.

6. Hold this position for time with as little movement as possible.

7. I generally begin with 10-15 seconds per side and progress up to 30 seconds per side. At this point, load can be incorporated by having the athlete hold a plate on their hips.

Side Plank

THE ALTERNATING FRONT PLANK

1. Set up in position to complete a front plank.

2. Contract right glute and lift right foot only 3-6 inches off of the floor to ensure the movement is coming from the hip versus from arching the low back.

3. Hold for 2 seconds.

4. Do not allow the body to rotate when the foot lifts.

5. Repeat on the left leg.

6. I generally prescribe this for 5-10 reps per side for a total of 20-40 seconds.

Alternating Front Plank

HIP MOBILITY

Much of this book has focused on actions occurring at or around the hip. In addition to being brutally strong, we also want the hips to have the ability to rotate, flex, and extend. As previously mentioned, this will not only have direct implications on the health of the lumbar spine, but will also directly impact the stability of the knee.

Remember: if the function of one joint is compromised, the surrounding joints will have to take over so that the movement can occur. With low back and knee health being major concerns in the sport of volleyball, the hips are of paramount importance.

But we need to recognize that *mobility* is the ability to *actively* move through ranges of motion, as opposed to *flexibility*, which is a more *passive* process. Many of the movements discussed in this book (full range of motion squatting, RDL variations) are training the hips' ability to flex, extend, and rotate without prescribing a special series of exercises. Too often, volleyball programs have fallen into the trap of worrying so much about mobility and flexibility that strength has been overlooked. This is flawed logic, as gaining strength in a specified range of motion leads to maintaining that ROM and sets the foundation for improving it.

Nonetheless, I will include a few hip mobility exercises in the training program, particularly as part of an athlete's warm-up or as a super-set between primary movements in the weight room. My two favorites are:

HIP FLEXOR STEP WITH ROTATION

1. Begin in the high plank position.

2. Step forward, placing the right foot next to and outside of the right hand so that the toes line up with the fingertips.

3. The back toe should remain pulled toward the shin and the back knee should be only slightly bent.

4. Lift the right arm off the ground and overhead where the fingers point towards the sky.

5. The eyes should follow the fingertips so that the neck and shoulders rotate towards the front leg (*bonus*: thoracic spine rotation).

6. Do not allow the arm to fall behind the midline of the body. Instead, actively reach up with the fingertips.

7. Replace the hand on the floor, step the right leg back into a high plank and repeat with the left side.

8. Complete 5 reps per side.

Hip Flexor Step with Rotation

90/90 SWITCHES (SHIN BOX)

1. Sit on the floor with the right hip externally rotated so the outside of the knee is on the floor. The knee should be bent to 90 degrees.

2. The left hip should be internally rotated with the inside of the knee on the floor. This knee is also bent to 90 degrees.

3. The shins should create a 90-degree angle relative to one another (hence the exercise's alias: "shin box").

4. Sit as tall as possible, with the shoulders square towards the right shin and the hands off of the floor.

5. Keeping the feet in place, lift both knees simultaneously and pivot across the feet so that the front leg becomes the back leg and vice versa.

6. The shoulders should move at the same pace as the knees and finish square towards the left shin.

7. The right hip will now finish in internal rotation and the left hip in external rotation.

8. Repeat by returning back to the starting position.

9. Do not allow the athletes to pick up their feet to complete the movement.

10. This movement should be completed under control. Do not allow the legs to "flop."

11. Complete 5 reps per side.

90/90 Switches (Setup)

90/90 Switches (Mid Range)

90/90 Switches (Finish)

THE KNEE

Though this book is focused on volleyball players, it is not necessarily focused solely on volleyball players who also happen to be female. Nonetheless, when the topic of injury reduction comes up relative to the knee, a relevant statistic is that females are 2 to 8 times more likely to tear their ACLs than their male counterparts.

Over the years *many* culprits have been pointed out: the Q-Angle, hormone fluctuations due to the menstrual cycle, and a more shallow femoral notch.

What is often swept under the rug is the fact that, in general, female athletes have less access to quality strength and conditioning programs than males. When they gain access, it often occurs at a later stage in development than their male counterparts. This is an uncomfortable truth because it is one the coaching community has control over. It is also one that very likely has a tremendous impact on the above-mentioned injury statistic.

While the other mentioned factors certainly contribute, things like anatomical differences and hormone profiles aren't within our control, so fretting about those isn't a good use of our time. Leave that to the researchers. While we may never know exactly *why* there's a problem, we must focus on *how* we're going to address the problem.

Just as with shoulder health, better knee health isn't as simple as adding a few cute prehab exercises to the training program. It IS the training program. Getting athletes stronger and more stable, teaching them to land and change directions, and managing their overall training volume will do more to reduce the likelihood of an ACL rupture than lateral band walks or other commonly prescribed exercises.

Truly important considerations relative to the health of an athlete's knee are:

- Single leg strength
- Eccentric control of the hamstring
- Hip and ankle mobility
- Trunk stability

The next step, then, is recognizing how those capacities directly relate to landing mechanics and change of direction.

Each of those capacities have already been covered at length in this book, except for ankle mobility.

ANKLE MOBILITY

Here's my patented (it's not patented) 5-step process for creating good ankle mobility with volleyball athletes without creating a separate program to do so:

1. Ankle braces during practice and games? Fine. Ankle braces during strength and conditioning? Nope.

2. Barefoot training when possible.
   a. Warm-ups.
   b. Extensive plyometrics.
   c. A-Series work.
   d. Some lifts *if* the setting allows it (never trust athletes to not chop their own toes off, or possibly someone else's, by dropping a weight in small spaces).

3. Squatting deep.

4. Getting strong/stable on a single leg.

5. Strengthening the ankle/calf complex.
   a. Barefoot training when possible (see above).
   b. Floating heel work.
   c. Ankle "CARs."

THE FLOATING HEEL ISO SPLIT SQUAT

Revisiting a condensed version of the Isometric Split Squat from Chapter 4:

1. Begin in a half-kneeling position.

2. Initiate the movement by lifting the back knee off the ground.

3. Once in position, "float" the front heel off the ground. I cue that there's an imaginary orange under the heel. Don't juice it.

4. Hold this position for 15-30 seconds.

Floating Heel ISO Split Squat

Incorporating this into your program is as simple as allocating 1-2 sets of iso split squats for the day to the floating heel position.

ANKLE CARs

The acronym CARs stands for "controlled articular rotations" and is part of Dr. Andreo Spina's Functional Range Conditioning system. The basic premise of a CAR is to rotate a joint through its largest range of motion while creating tension in that joint. This will strengthen the joint and improve its available range of motion over time.

One important element of a CAR is isolating movement to just the intended joint by tensioning the rest of the body.

Steps are as follows:

1. Sit on the ground, a box, or a bench.

2. Lift the right leg and hook the left arm under the right thigh behind the knee.

3. Place the right hand on the front of the right tibia to ensure that it does not rotate during the movement.

4. Take a deep breath and create tension throughout the entire body.

5. Hover the right foot off the ground and begin to "draw" the largest square possible with the toes by moving through the ankle.

6. Take 3 seconds to "draw" each side of the square and push hard when the corners are reached.

7. Complete 1-2 reps each clockwise and counterclockwise on each side as training time allows.

Ankle CARs (Setup)

This is an EXCELLENT thing to do daily in a pre-practice warm-up versus limiting it exclusively to a strength and conditioning setting.

INJURY REDUCTION – CLOSING THOUGHTS

In case you missed it, injury reduction is not the result of a separate program filled with pre-hab exercises. It is the product of the entire training program and should be viewed as such. Though the concepts and exercises presented in this chapter can be useful in the reduction of injury, I will reiterate that they are the icing on the cake–all but useless without the cake itself: the principles and methods comprising the other 14 chapters of this book.

SECTION 4:
PUTTING IT ALL TOGETHER – PROGRAM DESIGN

CHAPTER TWELVE:
PRINCIPLES OF PROGRAM DESIGN

There are entire books written on the topic of program design, but they all generally have the same flaw: they are written with the ideal situation in mind. These utopian programming guides generally include: an actual off-season, all the time in the world, an adequate coach to athlete ratio, and a facility with enough equipment to serve large groups of athletes.

As you are likely already painfully well aware, rarely if ever is the setting ideal, particularly in the middle and high school environment. Instead of walking in fresh and ready to train on a Monday, your athletes may be hobbling in after playing 753 sets of volleyball in a qualifier over the weekend. Or they may be multisport athletes who have a track meet in eleven days and the track coach, without consulting you, already informed them they need to rest. Textbook methods, while correct in theory, are rarely attainable in reality. Instead, we must design programs that are optimal given the context in which we train.

Without knowing every constraint that you face, I can't fully address what will be optimal in your specific situation; however, keep this overarching truth in mind when adapting these principles to your individual program:

By simply teaching athletes the basic movement patterns presented in this book, you are light years ahead of most programs. It's okay if the order isn't perfect, or if how you program the sets and reps isn't perfect, or if the equipment isn't perfect. If your athletes are executing movement patterns safely and effectively, they will get better and you're doing a great job as a coach.

With that being said, as we work through these principles, I will present a few workarounds for:

- Exercise order due to limited space/equipment
- Sets/reps

OVERALL SESSION STRUCTURE

Ideally, each session would be structured as follows:

1. Dynamic warm-up

2. Plyometrics

3.   Speed or Change of Direction

4.   Strength

5.   Conditioning

This doesn't mean each session needs to contain all five of these capacities, it's just the ideal order of operations for those capacities. Ideally, I would program numbers 1-4 on the same day of the week, but if you're doing only two or three due to time or facility constraints, simply do them in the listed order bypassing the ones that won't be included that day. In fact, a practical way to structure your training for the week is to use a dynamic warm-up, plyometrics, and speed/COD work as the first 15-20 minutes of your volleyball practice, with lifting occurring on a separate day.

But what about scenarios where the size of the facility or equipment limitations will not allow a large group of athletes to progress through the session in the order listed above? Simple...group your athletes by training age/developmental level. Provide priority access to the "correct" session order to those who have more experience training. Those of lower training ages will survive going out of order.

One caveat: *do not* mow athletes over with heavy lower body strength work or high intensity conditioning work prior to having them sprint or jump. If you're having to manipulate the order of the session, you may also need to manipulate the intensity of the session as a result.

Also, a good general rule of thumb is to not mow your athletes over in any one training session, *period*. Remember back to our second speed principle: "Don't let today's training session ruin tomorrow's." That can apply within a training session as well: don't let exercise A ruin exercise B.

DETERMINING THE SPEED OF PROGRESSION

Where it comes to writing training programs, everyone wants absolutes. They want principles like: "spend exactly this much time on this step of the progression, then move on to the next step."

I would love it if it were that simple. But learning isn't linear, and the human body is a bit more complex than that.

Nonetheless, here's a sample timeline for the speed of progression I use in the middle and high school setting, using the squat pattern as an example:

7th Grade	8th Grade	9th Grade	10th-12th Grade
6-12 Wks: CM Squat	2-6 Wks: CM Squat	2-6 Wks: CM Squat	BB Front Squat - % Based
6-12 Wks: Goblet Squat	2-6 Wks: Goblet Squat	2-6 Wks: Goblet Squat	
6-12 Wks: Hands-Free Front Squat	2 Wks: Hands-Free Front Squat	2 Wks: Hands-Free Front Squat	
CHRISTMAS BREAK	Barbell Front Squat	Barbell Front Squat	
2 Wks: CM Squat			
2 Wks: Goblet Squat			
6 Wks: Hands-Free Front Squat			
6 Wks: Barbell Front Squat			

Generally speaking, the younger the athlete, the more time we will spend at each step in the progression. Additionally, the more compliant athletes are with year-round training, the more likely they are to land on the shorter end of the suggested timeframe. As an example, an athlete finishing the 8th grade who transitions immediately to the incoming freshman summer program won't need to restart the training progression at Step 1. Conversely, an athlete who rolls up in August having never darkened the door of the gym over the summer will likely need to start from scratch–at least for a few weeks as they reacclimate to training.

Again, the table above provides a theoretical timeline for a squat progression, with other movements tracking similarly. The real-world timeline follows the path of this flow chart, with the speed of progression being dictated by an athlete's mastery of a given movement.

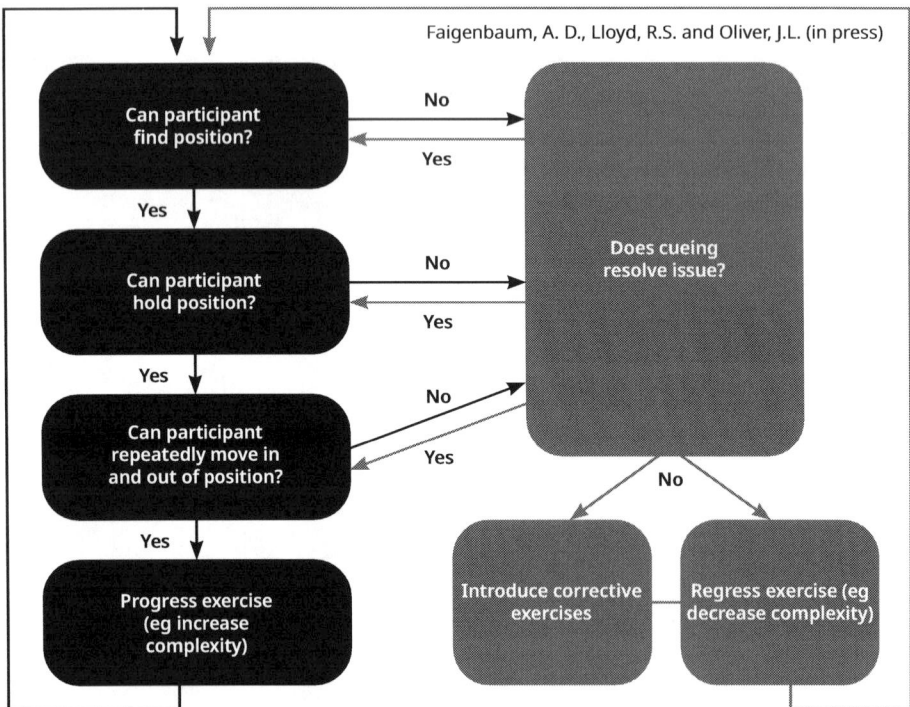

Faigenbaum, A. D., Lloyd, R.S. and Oliver, J.L. (in press)

But what if *most* of the athletes are ready to move on and just a few aren't? I use an 80/20 rule here. If 80% of the room "gets it" and can move forward, we move forward. The 20% who haven't yet mastered this step in the progression continue using it until they do.

"But Missy, shouldn't we progress each and every athlete at their own pace?"

Technically yes, but...

We are operating in the real world, where coach to athlete ratios are often less than ideal. It is incredibly difficult to execute 6 individualized programs in the same session, let alone 60.

Fortunately, by following the progressions outlined in the book, most of your athletes will be ready to move on at the same rate. The entire purpose of this book is to make your life easier as a coach, not to challenge you to attempt to run 60 different programs within a single training session–which is what the strength and conditioning industry would lead you to believe is the only "right" way.

To summarize: loosely follow the sample timeline above. If 80% of the group is ready to move on at the 6-week mark versus the 12-week mark? Then move on. Simple.

DETERMINING SETS AND REPS

When I first started writing training programs, I believed that sets and reps would determine the success or failure of the program. After designing and implementing thousands of training programs with developmental athletes, this has become the thing I spend the least amount of time worrying about.

Why? Because *everything* in the training program should be dictated by movement quality, not a predetermined number. Sets and reps will also be heavily influenced by how much time you have for the session and, keep in mind...most rep schemes will work with developmental athletes.

Because of those factors, sitting down and writing a section on the X's and O's of sets and reps for developmental athletes is actually quite challenging. These athletes are often a moving target, and I'm not in the room with you to see how they are progressing on a daily basis. The simplest, most important advice I would give to you as a coach is:

1. Don't sacrifice technique in an effort to complete a given number of reps. If you programmed 3 sets of 8 push-ups for your athletes that day and they can only do 3 sets of 4 push-ups? Then adjust the program to fit your group and set the goal of doing a fifth push-up the following week.

2. Don't sacrifice technique in an effort to move heavier weight. Developmental athletes will experience tremendous gains in strength using only submaximal weights! There is never a need to go to failure. My good friend Coach Monte Sparkman (who has squatted over 1000 pounds), told me he misses fewer than 2 reps per year in his own training. If an experienced, competitive powerlifter doesn't need to miss lifts to get stronger, rest assured a youth or adolescent volleyball player definitely doesn't need to either.

With all that being said, here are my general rules of thumb for reps per set:

EXERCISE TYPE	EXAMPLES	SETS	REP RANGE
Isometric	Iso split squat, plank	2-3	Timed Set: 10-60s
Eccentric	Ecc pull-up, Ecc push-up	2-3	1-6 reps (~3-30s ecc)
Bodyweight/Low Load	Vertical PVC RDL, CM Squat	2-4	5-10 reps
Loaded Primary Movement	BB Front Squat, BB RDL	3-6	2-5 reps
Auxiliary Movement	Y, T, Cobra, Glute Bridge	2-3	6-12 reps

As far as intensity goes, I let the athlete's technique dictate the weight. A really simple way of programming is to add 2.5-5 lbs per week as the athlete becomes stronger and the movement becomes more fluid. However, basic math tells us you can't continue to add 2.5-5 lbs a week throughout the athlete's career. This is where understanding *relative intensity* becomes important.

Though there are flaws in this system (as there are with any system), I think Prilepin's Chart is an outstanding resource to use when learning to write training programs. This table shows how sets, reps, and percentages (intensity) relate to one another and how to prescribe them to optimize strength adaptations.

PERCENT OF 1RM	REPS/SETS	OPTIMAL # OF REPS	TOTAL REP RANGE
55-65	3-6	24	18-30
70-80	3-6	18	12-24
80-90	2-4	15	10-20
90+	1-2	4	10

As it pertains to beginner athletes, coaches should note that Prilepin's Chart was established based on competitive weightlifters. That knowledge, coupled with the time constraints we're generally under during a training session with developmental athletes, leads me to err on the low end of the chart's rep range when programming.

Additionally, you don't have to test 1 rep maxes or use percentages at all. Prilepin's Chart can be extrapolated using Rate of Perceived Exertion (RPE) by approximating an RPE of 10 with 100%, RPE 9 of 90%, and so on. RPE can also be estimated using "reps in reserve" (RIR), or how many additional reps an athlete feels they *could* complete after completing the prescribed reps for the set.

RPE Scale Based on Reps in Reserve
RPE 10 = no more reps could be completed
RPE 9 = 1 more rep could be completed
RPE 8 = 2 more reps could be completed
RPE 7 = 3 more reps could be completed
RPE 5-6 = 4-6 more reps could be completed
RPE 1-4 = very light effort

While a percentage-based system has the flaw of relying upon some form of testing in order to establish training loads, the RPE/RIR system is flawed because it relies upon athlete self-awareness.

Because all systems are flawed, to establish intensity, one of the best tools you can use is your coach's eye. Ask yourself these two questions when observing athletes during training sessions:

1. *Is the movement technically sound?*

2. *Does the athlete appear to be working at the desired intensity?*

Prescribed numbers get you in the ballpark, but a good coach's eye will help you throw strikes.

CHAPTER THIRTEEN:
PROGRAMMING PHASE 1

Coaches much more creative than I have catchy phrases for the levels of their training program, like Joe Kenn's "Block Zero" or Zach Dechant's "Positions Block." I'm not as creative, so I just call phase one of my training program "Phase 1."

In Phase 1, we want to begin teaching athletes the five basic movement patterns detailed in Section 2. Given that these movement patterns will likely be completely new to your athletes, you want to expose them to the movements as often as possible. Think of it like math class: if you want to learn math, you do it every day. Movement is no different.

Daily practice of basic movement patterns represents the ideal circumstance. But, as I believe I mentioned, it isn't an ideal world... so let's discuss optimal. At a *bare minimum*, you should expose your athletes to these movements twice a week. If you can train more frequently than that, you will see gains more quickly. But I'm 100% about practicality and I understand that allocating 5 days a week to strength and conditioning isn't a sustainable model for most programs.

The general daily template for Phase 1 is as follows, with suggestions in the gray boxes for structuring group training sessions:

PHASE 1 PROGRAM TEMPLATE	
Dynamic Warm-Up Extensive Plyometrics & Jumps (landing emphasis) A-Series Work or* UAP Steps on Whistle Accelerations or* The Grid	
Tiers 1&2: Athletes in Groups of 3 to 4 (if 4 - Athlete 4 is assigned rest)	
1a.	Squat Pattern
1b.	Athlete Coaching Squat Pattern
1c.	Plank Variation
2a.	Hip Hinge
2b.	Athlete Coaching Hip Hinge
2c.	Upper Body Pull (horizontal only)
Tier 3: All Athletes Perform All Exercises Together	
3a.	Upper Body Push
3b.	Single Leg
3c.	Glute Bridge
3d.	Scapular Stability

*Choice will depend on whether you want the session to have a linear speed focus, or a change of direction focus.

While it can be tempting for purposes of brevity–or, from the perspective of "conditioning"–to view the above template as circuit training, that is not its intent. Great care should be taken to ensure that athletes aren't doing too much in the initial phases of learning. In fact, quite often during the first few sessions I train a team, we may only make it through 1a-1c. I would rather allocate time to coaching and correcting a few movements than rush the process and lay a poor foundation for multiple movements.

Don't feel like you have to complete everything you have written out for the day. Instead, monitor and preserve movement quality at all times and at all cost. This practice will pay dividends later in the training process. Again, our emphasis here is teaching proper movement patterns, not following a specific recipe. Be a chef, not a cook.

Something else that can tremendously assist the process of instilling proper movement patterns is teaching athletes to coach one another. To do this, I provide them with 2-3 easy to identify cues to look for in a given movement and show them exactly where to stand and what it looks like to be actively engaged while coaching their teammate. This provides a number of benefits:

- Keeps everyone actively engaged in the session. Coaches hate standing around, so much so that many will sacrifice session quality to avoid it. Having athletes coach one another is a wonderful compromise–they are mentally engaged while physically resting.
- Deploys a fleet of cooks to help the chef. I can't coach every single rep any more than the head chef can prepare and plate every meal at a restaurant. But with a team of athletes helping me? Multiple courses of coaching cues are served.
- Develops athletes who are willing to give and receive feedback from teammates without taking it personally.
- Heightens awareness of one's own movements. After spending a set correcting their teammate's movements, this should translate to the athlete being more cognizant of their own.

With this in mind and using the Phase 1 Program Template above, here is what a training day might look like for an athlete in this phase:

	DEVELOPMENTAL VOLLEYBALL ATHLETE PHASE I	Week 1	Week 2	Week 3	Week 4	Week 5	Week 6
	Dynamic Warm-Up	3-5 min					
	Jog	20 yards					
	Backpedal	20 yards					
	Upper Body Clamshell	5 each side					
	Lateral Shuffle with Overhead Swing (right)	20 yards					
	Lateral Shuffle with Overhead Swing (left)	20 yards					
	Hip Flexor Step with rotation	5 each side					
	Extensive Plyometrics and Jumps						
	Pogo Hops in Place	3x15					
	Jumps to Box (stick and hold landing in UAP - 2 seconds)	3x3					
	Speed Development or Change of Direction						
	A Series Drills (2-3 Variations)	15 yds each					
	10 Yard Accelerations	6-10 reps					
1a	**Squat Progression - USE SQUAT WEDGE**	2x5	3x5	3x5	3x5	4x5	4x5
	Wk 1-2: Countermovement Squat (3-2-1 tempo)						
	Wk 3-6: Goblet Squat (3-2-1 tempo)						
1b	**Coach Your Teammate!**						
	Cues: Feet flat, torso vertical, hamstring on calf						
1c	**Front Plank**	2x20s	3x20s	3x30s	3x40s	3x45s	3x50s
2a	**RDL Progression**	2x8	3x8	3x5	3x5	3x5	3x5
	Wk 1-2: Vertical PVC RDL						
	Wk 3-6: Horizontal PVC RDL or BB RDL (can start with lighter bar)						
2b	**Coach Your Teammate!**						
	Cues: Feet hip distance, slight knee bend, 3 points of contact w/PVC						
2c	**Reverse Pullup Progression**	2x15s	3x15s	3x5	3x5	3x5	3x5
	Wk 1-2: Iso Holds (top position for time)						
	Wk 3-6: Eccentric Reverse Pull-Up (5 second eccentric - add 1s every 2 weeks)						
3a	**Pushup Progression**	2x30s	3x30s	3x5	3x5	3x6	3x6
	Wk 1-2: High Plank						
	Wk 3-6: Eccentric Push-Up (hands elevated as needed) 5 second eccentric						
3b	**Iso Split Squat**	2x10s ea	3x10s ea	3x15s ea	3x18s ea	3x20s ea	3x20s ea
	Wk 1-3: All sets front foot flat						
	WK 4-6: Floating heel on Set 3						
3c	**2 Part Glute Bridge**	2x8	3x8	3x8	3x30s	3x45s	3x60s
	Wk 1-3: 2 second hold at top						
	Wk 4-6: Isometric glute bridge						
3d	**Prone Y & T**	2x10s ea	3x10s ea	3x12s ea	3x12s ea	3x15s ea	3x15s ea
	Hold Y for prescribed time then transition to T held for time						

To reiterate an important concept: the younger an athlete is and/ or the less training experience they have, the longer they will spend at any given step in the progression. The example above is copied directly from the first 6 weeks of my freshman volleyball training program at Byron Nelson High School. In this specific situation, being an incoming high school freshman meant they already had two prior years of exposure to some of these movements during their time at our two feeder middle schools. As a result, we were able to move through these movements more quickly (over a period of 6 weeks), than if they'd arrived on campus with no prior experience. To drive this point home, while those same athletes were 7th or 8th graders, they typically spent an entire semester working through only what is listed in the program above.

Additionally, as a point of reference, a session like the one listed above generally took around 40-45 minutes to complete with a group of 30 athletes working three to a rack in the weight room. If you only have 30-35 minutes, you can divide the session and complete the plyometrics and speed or COD work on a different day of the week, potentially as a warm-up to a volleyball skill session.

CHAPTER FOURTEEN:
PROGRAMMING PHASE 2

The purpose of Phase 2 is to continue working through the various progressions and to begin increasing load. Again, the length of time spent at each step of the progression will be dictated by athlete readiness. As a reminder: it is never acceptable to add load at the expense of technique simply to chase numbers in the weight room. However, you are doing your athletes a disservice by not getting them in the weight room and getting them stronger. Walking the line between these two ends of the spectrum is another instance where using your coach's eye instead of attempting to copy and paste a training program becomes critical.

In particular during Phase 2, you may start to notice that different exercises have different rates of progression. A typical example of this is that athletes with long limbs may struggle with push-ups and pull-ups, but be readily able to move additional weight on RDLs. I cannot tell you what that will look like for every team or every athlete. Determine when to progress by using your best judgment based on what you've learned thus far regarding appropriate technique.

The overall template of Phase 2 will seem extremely familiar. Remember: the goal is to master the basic movement patterns learned in Phase 1. Once these are mastered, coaches and athletes can successfully add more variety into a training program because the foundational principles are the same for most exercises!

PHASE 1 PROGRAM TEMPLATE	
Dynamic Warm-Up Extensive Plyometrics & Jumps A-Series Work & Speed or UAP Work & Change of Direction	
Athletes in groups of 3-4	
1a.	Squat Pattern
1b.	Athlete Coaching Squat Pattern
1c.	Scapular Stability
2a.	Hip Hinge
2b.	Crawling Pattern
2c.	Upper Body Pull (horizontal or vertical)
3a.	Upper Body Push
3b.	Single Leg
3c.	Plank Variation

More specifically, a sample day for Phase 2 could look like this:

	DEVELOPMENTAL VOLLEYBALL ATHLETE PHASE II	Week 1	Week 2	Week 3	Week 4	Week 5	Week 6
	Dynamic Warm-Up	3-5 min					
	Extensive Plyometrics and Jumps						
	Rudiments (Locomotive) - Fwd, Bwd, Lateral	3x15 yards					
	Box Step-off (stick and hold in UAP 2 seconds)	2x3					
	Lateral Box Jump (stick and hold in UAP 2 seconds)	2x3					
	Speed Development or Change of Direction						
	A Series Drills (2-3 Variations)	15 yds each					
	Acceleration - 10-20 yards (vary starting position)	80-100yds					
1a	**Squat Progression - USE SQUAT WEDGE AS NEEDED**	3x4	3x4	3x5	3x5	4x5	4x5
	Wk 1-2: Hands Free BB Front Squat (3-2-1 Tempo)						
	Wk 3-6: BB Front Squat (3-2-1 Tempot)						
1b	**Coach Your Teammate!**						
	Cues: Feet flat, torso vertical, hamstring on calf						
1c	**Incline Cobra**	3x10	3x10	3x12	3x12	3x15	3x15
2a	**BB RDL**	2x5	3x5	3x5	3x5	3x5	3x5
2b	**Leopard Crawl Spelling Bee (Spell 5-7 letters)**	2 sets	3 sets	3 sets	3 sets	3 sets	3 sets
2c	**Reverse Pullup Progression**	2x5	3x4	3x5	3x3	3x3	3x3
	Week 1-3: Eccentric Reverse Pull-Up (5s eccentric)						
	Wk 4-6: Iso + Eccentric Reverse Pull-Up (5 second iso, 5 second eccentric)						
3a	**Pushup Progression**						
	Eccentric Push-up (elevate hands on an as needs basis)	2x5	3x5	3x5	3x6	3x6	3x6
	WEEK 1 - 5 second eccentric. Add 1 second every two weeks						
3b	**Split Squat Progression**	2x5e	3x5e	3x5e	3x5e	3x5e	3x5e
	Week 1-2: Bottom Up Split Squat						
	Week 3-6: Top Down Eccentric Split Squat (3s eccentric)						
3c	**Side Plank**	2x15s	3x15s	3x20s	3x25s	3x30s	3x30s

From a frequency standpoint, the ideal scenario would be three higher intensity days–such as the one listed above–with two lower intensity days in between. This means that unless there is a special circumstance demanding otherwise (like a Monday–Thursday summer training schedule), I will always plan sessions to be total body. The reasons for this are:

1. We are training athletes, not working in bodybuilding splits. The sport of volleyball is played with both the upper and lower body simultaneously and training should reflect that.

2. Stress consolidation. Rather than having four high volume/ intensity days in a row, I would rather have a high stress day followed by a low stress day in order to facilitate recovery and set the stage for success in the next higher intensity day.

A Phase 2 week might be planned as follows:

DAY	INTENSITY LEVEL
MONDAY	HIGH
TUESDAY	LOW
WEDNESDAY	HIGH
THURSDAY	LOW
FRIDAY	HIGH
SATURDAY	OFF
SUNDAY	OFF

However, if you've worked with volleyball for any length of time, you recognize that the above scenario is *rarely* reality. While I would love for your athletes to have a dedicated off-season in which to develop, I'm also here to give you the tools you need to help your athletes be successful in the real world.

Real world sample weeks go as follows:

HIGH SCHOOL TOURNAMENT WEEK	
DAY	INTENSITY LEVEL
MONDAY	LOW
TUESDAY	MATCH
WEDNESDAY	LOW OR OFF DUE TO TRAVEL
THURSDAY	TOURNAMENT
FRIDAY	TOURNAMENT
SATURDAY	TOURNAMENT
SUNDAY	OFF

HIGH SCHOOL REGULAR SEASON (2 GAMES PER WEEK)	
DAY	INTENSITY LEVEL
MONDAY	LOW
TUESDAY	MATCH
WEDNESDAY	LOW/MODERATE
THURSDAY	MODERATE
FRIDAY	MATCH
SATURDAY	LOW/MODERATE
SUNDAY	OFF

CLUB TOURNAMENT WEEK	
DAY	INTENSITY LEVEL
MONDAY	LOW OR OFF
TUESDAY	MODERATE/HIGH
WEDNESDAY	LOW
THURSDAY	LOW OR OFF DUE TO TRAVEL
FRIDAY	TOURNAMENT
SATURDAY	TOURNAMENT
SUNDAY	TOURNAMENT

Given those schedules, you can quickly see that the perfect five day high/low system is a challenge, to say the least. Further complicating matters is the fact that within a given training session, you may have the following:

- ⅓ of your athletes who played in a club tournament the previous weekend.
- ⅓ of your athletes with a tournament coming up this weekend.
- ⅓ of your athletes who are more than one week pre/post tournament.

These three statuses present widely different training needs. So how does a coach address all of these needs simultaneously and accommodate for the many stressors outside of the strength and conditioning programming?

By a show of hands.

Prior to the start of an early-week session, I ask athletes to raise their hands if they played in a tournament the previous weekend. (Usually this is just a formality, as I know who had a tournament by watching them limp through the door.) In mid- to late-week sessions, I'll ask for a show of hands of who will be playing a tournament this upcoming weekend. Based on the responses, I will put athletes into one of three categories, named after my favorite source of protein: *steak*.

Not only is steak an elite source of protein, perhaps the *only* thing that the strength and conditioning industry will agree upon is our sacred mantra: *don't burn the steak*. Some readers may find this phrase silly or unnecessary. Strength coaches do not. We're dead serious: **don't burn** *a steak*. EVER. It's an absolute travesty and is completely avoidable. If a steak is undercooked, you can always throw it back on the grill to cook a bit longer. However, once a steak is cooked past the desired level of doneness, it cannot be undone. This is EXACTLY how we need to think of the accumulation of stress across an athlete's training week (and for that matter, their career) and then plan accordingly. You can always add, but you can never take away.

The following table shows what qualifies an athlete to be in a given category, and how I adjust their training accordingly:

TIMELINE	STEAK TEMP	VOLUME	INTENSITY	OTHER
• Post Break +1-2 Wks • Gameday +/- 1 Day • Pre-season Camps	Rare (low day)	50-60% of planned session or max volume	50-75% or 5-7 RPE or 3-6 RIR	Consider using regressed movement to ↓ stress
• Early Off-season • Gameday +/- 2 Days	Medium rare (moderate day)	75-80% of planned session/max volume	65-85% or 6-8 RPE or 2-4 RIR	Prilepin low, low volume speed/plyo/COD
• Late Off-season • Gameday +/- 3 Days	Medium/ Med. Well (high day)	100% of planned session/max volume	70-95% or 7-9 RPE or 1-3 RIR	Prilepin optimal, low-moderate volume speed/plyo/COD

By using the above "steak temperature" parameters and the sample weekly schedules presented previously, volume and intensity can be planned for each session during a given week. The programming template for Phase 2 can serve as a high, moderate, or low day, depending on how you manipulate the variables listed above.

For example, the squat pattern could be assigned as follows to a group of athletes with different needs. The high day represents what is "planned," while the moderate and low days show the modifications based on athlete readiness or time of year:

- High Day – Barbell Front Squat at 7-9 RPE or 70-90% – 5 sets
- Medium Day – Barbell Front Squat at 6-8 RPE or 65-80% – 3 sets
- Low Day – Barbell Front Squat at 5-7 RPE or 50-70% OR Goblet Squat – 2 sets

You might feel overwhelmed knowing you need to make adjustments for multiple athletes in the same session, but the above guidelines make it really simple. You don't need to write multiple programs, you just need to modify the existing program to address multiple different needs.

Modifications like:

- Those with a tournament tomorrow do two sets of everything instead of four.
- Those with a tournament tomorrow do goblet squats instead of barbell front squats.

Simple. Easy. Effective.

If you have situations where you feel that even these modifications won't facilitate sufficient recovery and you have enough coaches or team leadership to execute this, another option is to substitute a recovery session for the day's planned training session. A session composed of a dynamic warm-up, 3-5 mobility/stability exercises from Section 3, and the low intensity cardiac output circuit presented in Chapter 10 functions beautifully in this scenario.

Here's what a sample training week using this intervention might look like during club season for a player who participated in a tournament the previous weekend:

MONDAY	TUESDAY	WEDNESDAY	THURSDAY	FRIDAY
• Warm-Up • Mobility Exercises • Cardiac Output Circuit	• Skill Day	• Warm-Up • COD/Plyos • Lift	• Skill Day	• Warm-Up • Speed/Plyos • Lift

And a sample week for a player with a tournament at the end of the week:

MONDAY	TUESDAY	WEDNESDAY	THURSDAY	FRIDAY
• Warm-Up • Speed/Plyos • Lift	• Skill Day	• Warm-Up • COD/Plyos • Lift	• Skill Day	• Warm-Up • Mobility • Cardiac Output Circuit

And one for a player with no tournament:

MONDAY	TUESDAY	WEDNESDAY	THURSDAY	FRIDAY
• Warm-Up • Speed/Plyos • Lift	• Skill Day	• Warm-Up • COD/Plyos • Lift	• Skill Day	• Warm-Up • Speed/Plyos • Lift

Again, there is no need to write three different programs, just execute one program three different ways.

CHAPTER FIFTEEN:
PROGRAMMING PHASE 3

Spoiler Alert: Phase 3 will include many of the same movements as Phases 1&2. I'm 41-years-old at the time of writing this, and I still use basic movements like goblet squats, barbell RDLs, and reverse pull-ups in my own program despite training for more than 25 years.

However, if after reaching this point in the book you still think your athletes are too advanced for the basics of S&C, that's okay. In fact, let's adjust your volleyball practice plans to match. Moving forward, I want you to replace *all* serve receive practice with one-off special situation training. Your team is clearly too elite to be bothered with fundamentals.

Not a good idea? Neither is trying to get fancy with strength and conditioning.

The basics work, and they work really well. There is not often a need to eliminate them from a training program. Rarely (read: never) will you work with a middle or high school athlete too advanced for these methods. In truth, there is nothing I've presented in this book that didn't comprise about 80% of the training program I used with Division I volleyball players (hence the book's title). The difference typically lies in the speed of progression.

Nonetheless, Phase 3 brings with it two key changes:

1.   A wider variety of movements.

2.   The prescription of load.

Once I'm confident that movements are mastered, we broaden the movement vocabulary and begin to pursue strength and power. By *mastered*, I mean that an athlete looks the same under a 5 pound squat or a 500 pound squat because the expectations are clear and the technique is ingrained.

MOVEMENT VARIETY

To reiterate, rarely–if ever–will we stray completely from the basic movements detailed in previous chapters. However, the inclusion of additional exercises allows us to:

- *Provide a different training stimulus to the body.* In truth, us mere mortals cannot just increase load ad infinitum. Were that the case, the world would be filled with 1,000 pound squatters like my friend Monte. By adding different movement patterns into a program, we can challenge athletes without necessarily increasing load.
- *Train in multiple planes of movement.* Thus far, we have primarily focused on movements occurring in the sagittal plane. However, volleyball is played in all three planes of movement, which are shown in the figure below.

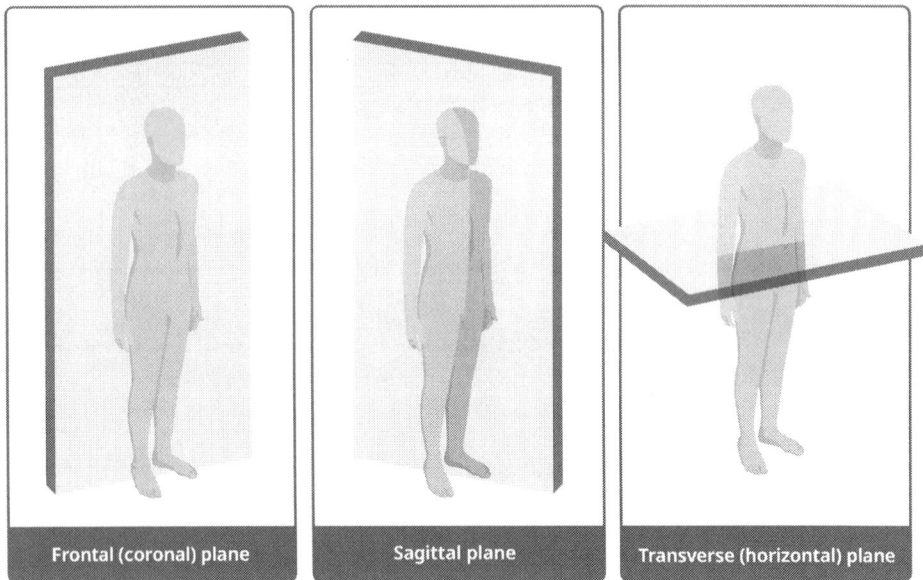

| Frontal (coronal) plane | Sagittal plane | Transverse (horizontal) plane |

Sample movements in each plane are as follows:

FRONTAL PLANE	SAGITTAL PLANE	TRANSVERSE PLANE
Lateral Lunge	Reverse Lunge	Transverse Lunge
Lateral Box Jump	Forward Box Jump	90 Degree Turn Box Jump
Med Ball Side Toss	Med Ball Backward OH Throw	Medball Bwd OH Rotational Throw

I begin incorporating multiple planes in Phase 2 of training (particularly in our speed/COD/plyometric work), but place a heavier emphasis on it in Phase 3 as I feel the basics have been mastered and no longer need to consume the entire training session.

- *Increase athlete engagement through variety*. Real talk: training can be really boring. Sometimes you have to throw athletes a bone. Changing up exercises can do exactly that.

With that being said...the overall structure of the workout won't often change and in order to actually see adaptations from a given exercise, you need to incorporate it over the course of many weeks. Variety for the sake of engagement is not a free pass to cast aside the well-designed training methodology detailed thus far in favor of the CrossFit or group fitness workout you did this morning, or whatever it is you did *back in the day*. Simply place additional exercises in the existing templates shown in Phases 1 and 2.

Here's how that might look:

DEVELOPMENTAL VOLLEYBALL ATHLETE PHASE III		Week 1	Week 2	Week 3	Week 4	Week 5	Week 6
	Dynamic Warm-Up						
	Extensive Plyometrics and Jumps						
	Rudiments (Locomotive) - Lateral Switches, Single Leg Medial, Single Leg Lateral	3x15 yards					
	90-Degree Jump to Box	2x2e					
	Drop Jump to Lateral Hurdle Hop	2x3e					
	Speed Development or Change of Direction						
	A Series Drills (2-3 Drill Variation)	15yds each					
	Timed 10 Yard Fly (5-10 yard fly in zone)	~80-100yds					
1a	**BB Front Squat (Modified 5-3-1 Program)**	5+ week	3+ week	1+ week	5+	3+	1+
	Squat wedge as needed						
1b	**Coach Your Teammate!**						
	Cues: Feet flat, torso vertical, hamstring on calf						
1c	**Incline Y, T, Cobra**	3x5e	3x5e	3x5e	3x5e	3x5e	3x5e
2a	**BB RDL - HEAVY (↑ 5-10lbs a week as technique allows)**	3x5	3x5	3x5	3x5	3x5	3x5
2b	**Rest**						
2c	**TRX Row**						
	2-Arm Concentric, 1-Arm Eccentric (3 second eccentric)	3x5e	3x5e	3x5e	3x5e	3x5e	3x5e
3a	**Push-Up to Rotation**	3x5e	3x5e	3x5e	3x6e	3x6e	3x6e
3b	**Lateral Goblet Lunge**	3x5e	3x5e	3x5e	3x6e	3x6e	3x6e
3c	**Dead Bug with Single-Arm Dumbbell Reach**	3x5e	3x5e	3x5e	3x6e	3x6e	3x6e

Coaches need to understand that the above training session is an example of using the same overall template with added variety, rather than a blanket prescription. As a result, some of the exercises that appear will not have been covered in this text.

MOVEMENT VARIETY CONTINUED – THE OLYMPIC LIFTS

To be clear: yes, I do believe in using the Olympic lifts in training athletes. But three boxes must be checked in order for me to incorporate them in a training program:

First, and most importantly, the coach needs to be proficient at teaching them. If you feel even a moment's hesitation about your ability to teach them, DO NOT include them in an athlete's training program. Ever. If you don't feel competent yet–but do feel compelled to learn–enroll in a USA Weightlifting course.

Second, there needs to be time available to teach and implement the Olympic lifts. Many struggle to find time to get their athletes proficient at movements like the hip hinge and squat pattern. If that describes your situation? You might steer clear of trying to use Olympic lifts in your training program, since the hinge and squat are prerequisites for the safe implementation of these lifts.

Finally, some level of athleticism is required to learn these lifts. Not every "athlete" is athletic enough to perform them correctly, and that's okay. Fit the training program to the athlete, not the athlete to the training program.

But given that the strength and conditioning industry has long praised the Olympic lifts as the best way to train athletes, this begs the question:

If not the Olympic lifts, how do we develop explosive power?

It comes down to this: increasing force production (covered in Section 2: Basic Movement Patterns and Progressions) and learning to apply that force (covered in Section 3: Speed, Plyometrics, & Change of Direction.)

This can be done with or without the Olympic lifts.

Using the Olympic lifts, I've trained volleyball programs and athletes that won State Championships; and, without using the Olympic lifts, I've trained volleyball programs and athletes that won State Championships. The methods for success may differ (Oly lifts vs plyometrics and medicine ball throws), as long as the principles remain intact (force production/application).

PRESCRIPTION OF LOAD

Another key difference in Phase 3 of training is the prescription of load. Rather than letting athletes self-select weights, I prescribe weights for them based on percentages of a projected max. The benefits are as follows:

1. It keeps little Susie and little Jamal from coming in and loading the same sad 10 lbs on each side of the bar from now until all eternity.

2. It keeps their possibly more annoying counterparts, big Alexis and big Daniel, from coming in and trying to 1 rep max every session because that's what they did with Dad this weekend and they want to try 5 more pounds.

Basically, it allows **you** to control one more variable of training, which potentially gets you closer to the desired goal.

However, there are two major drawbacks to using percentage based loads:

1. 80% may not be 80% *today*. With young athletes, you're working with a moving target. They may get rapidly stronger, and 80% is actually 70% that day and they aren't being taxed enough. On the other hand, they may have hit a growth spurt and 80% is actually 95%, given that they haven't adapted to their newly increased limb length or altered center of mass. Or they may be coming off of a tournament, in which 80% is actually 137% because they are exhausted.

2. You need some type of starting point (a 1 rep max or estimated 1RM) to base percentages off of.

ESTABLISHING A 1 REP MAX OR ESTIMATED 1 REP MAX

At one time in my career, I was that traditional coach. We had to max out. I had to have a 1RM or it would be *impossible* for me to determine appropriate training loads. Unfortunately, with max out days came atrocious technique in order to pursue 5-10 more pounds. Eventually, growing tired of these harrowing displays, I pivoted. I put incredibly tight parameters in place. We effectively ran testing days like a powerlifting meet–with depth requirements, up calls, etc.

While technique during testing sessions improved to some extent, there was still a good bit of "creative license" taken by the coaching staff assisting in the session to ensure the kids went up in weight. At times, this produced numbers with the accuracy of a game of darts in the dark.

Even more disturbing than some questionable numbers, this protocol was a MASSIVE time suck. It would sometimes take an entire training session to collect data on a single lift, and 1-2 weeks to gather all relevant data. During this time, athletes were completing maybe 10 total reps a day and doing very little other training. With time being of the essence, I pivoted again.

Enter the 3RM era of my coaching career. This would solve EVERYTHING! Or, so I thought.

Unfortunately, what it actually did was produce all of the previously-mentioned problems while simultaneously taking *even longer* for kids to figure out what a 3RM should look and feel like. As an added bonus, after the session ended, I had to take the time to convert these inaccurate 3RMs into even less accurate 1RMs. Hooray!!

Listen, I'm not here to tell you not to use either of these two methods. I did for many years and still would in a few select circumstances. But here's the system I transitioned into:

ESTIMATED 1RM VIA REVERSE-ENGINEERED REPS IN RESERVE

Recall back to Chapter 12, where we discussed reps in reserve. A true reps in reserve system tells an athlete something along the lines of:

"For a set of 5, select a weight that you feel that you could successfully complete 7 reps with."

AKA: 2 reps in reserve.

I have found the traditional reps in reserve system to end up in yet another situation where our dear friends little Susie & Jamal, along with big Alexis & Daniel, all show up to the party even though no one invited them.

For a set of 5 with 2 reps in reserve, here's how it typically goes down:

- The Susies and Jamals lift what would be roughly 9 reps in reserve, feigning complete exhaustion.
- The Alexises and Daniels get stapled by the bar after 2 reps, clocking in at negative three reps in reserve, then demand the chance to try again. *"I got this Coach!"*
- Coach Missy is big mad because apparently no one heard her obviously stellar instructions, and she's storming around in a huff–taking weights off of Alexis's bar and adding them onto Susie's bar while Daniel and Jamal try to blend into the wall.

To send this unwanted crew packing–and to avoid smoke rolling out of my ears–I flipped the reps in reserve equation. To do this, I started with a prescribed weight and upon completion of the set, asked athletes how many additional reps they felt like they could complete. It might look like this:

- 5 reps at 100 lbs.
- Athlete feels they could have completed 2 additional reps.
- 100 lbs = 7RM (5 reps completed + 2 reps in reserve = 7RM).

From there, one can calculate an estimated 1RM (E1RM). Several formulas exist to convert rep maxes to E1RMs. To be honest, I couldn't care less which specific one gets used since they will all get you inside the ballpark, but I use the Epley formula:

(.0333 x reps x weight) + weight = Estimated 1RM

So in the above example:

(.0333 x 7 x 100) + 100 = 123 lbs

The athlete's E1RM is *123 lbs*, which I round to *125 lbs*.

I have athletes complete this *every* session where load is prescribed. This system solves a number of problems:

1. It doesn't take away from training time like dedicated testing days do. We are simply training and collecting data each session. The training is the testing and the testing is the training.

2. Loads are modified *weekly* instead of every 6 weeks. This allows us to look at trends over time, rather than just a few snapshots in time. It also adapts to an athlete's state of readiness on a daily/weekly basis, rather than assuming that every single day they walk in equally ready to train.

3. After the initial learning curve, it gives just about the same number you might arrive at with 1RM testing. In truth, it's probably a more accurate number to use in training because technique was better and the drama and hype of a max day was removed.

However, two problems are created using this system:

1. You can very clearly see that there will be work on the back-end for you as a coach. You have to collect and input data in order to calculate the adjusted E1RM, then calculate percentages based off of that. I would *strongly* recommend athlete management software for the weight room if you go this route, unless you want to become best friends with Excel. If the acquisition of software isn't affordable in your setting, there is nothing wrong with only collecting data once every 6 or so weeks. Do what is practical and sustainable in your setting.

2. As mentioned, the drama and hype of max day are *removed*. This causes cognitive dissonance for some coaches, who tend to rebut with:

    "But kids love it!!"

They also love vaping and eating pizza for breakfast, but are those the best choices? I'll leave the answer up to you!

"But _____ (Culture!!/MENTAL TOUGHNESS!!!)"

Neither of these things are trained or built in a single day or even in a few days. They are a product of consistently doing what is required day in and day out. They will be much more effectively addressed using the system above than relegating them to one testing day every 6-12 weeks in the off-season.

"We need to give them a chance to compete!!"

A chance to compete? Surely you jest. Are volleyball players not provided with sufficient opportunities to compete in the 7,000 games they play during their year-round competitive season? Is it competitive event number 7,001 (the poorly executed 1RM) that tips the scales in your team's favor?

As you can see by my addendums to the rebuttals of 1RM enthusiasts, those rebuttals don't hold water in my book. The benefits of using the E1RM system I've just described far outweigh the costs, and outweigh any perceived benefits of true max days.

USING THE E1RM TO DETERMINE LOADS

The number of set and rep schemes you will find during even a cursory Google search is massive. To try to teach them to you in a chapter section, entire chapter, or even an entire book would be a daunting task. Fortunately, everything works from a set and rep standpoint provided that:

1. Technique is not compromised by chasing more weight or additional reps.

2. Loads are prescribed somewhere within range of Prilepin's Chart outlined in Chapter 12.

3. There is some progression in weight over time.

Given that, I'm going to briefly describe how I have modified what I found to be one of the most effective systems for developing strength with Phase 3 athletes: Jim Wendler's 5-3-1 program. It is important to note that you should *only* begin implementing this system when you are confident that athletes are able to withstand heavier loads because you have taken the time to progress up to this point during Phase 2.

Traditionally, the Wendler 5-3-1 program looks like this:

WENDLER'S ORIGINAL 5-3-1 PROGRAM				
WEEK	REP SCHEME	WORK SET 1	WORK SET 2	WORK SET 3
1	5/5/5+	65% x5	75% x5	85% x5+
2	3/3/3+	70% x3	80% x3	90% x3+
3	5/3/1+	75% x5	85% x3	95% x1+
4	Deload	40% x5	50% x5	60% x5

Percentages here are based off of a "training max" which was 90% of an actual 1RM. Plus sets, indicated by the (+) symbol, are designed to have athletes do as many reps as they are able to at the prescribed weight without reaching failure, or always feeling they could compete one additional rep.

My modifications are as follows:

MODIFIED 5-3-1- PROGRAM					
WEEK	REP SCHEME	WORK SET 1	WORK SET 2	WORK SET 3	PLUS SET
1	5/5/5/5+*	65% x5	75% x5	85% x5	? x5
2	3/3/3/3+*	70% x3	80% x3	90% x3	? x3
3	5/3/1/1+*	75% x5	85% x3	95% x1	? x1
4	5/5/5/5+*	65% x5	75% x5	85% x5	? x5
5	3/3/3/3+*	70% x3	80% x3	90% x3	? x3
6	5/3/1/1+*	75% x5	85% x3	95% x1	? x1

1. Instead of the third work set being an opportunity to complete as many reps as possible, I use the third work set as an indicator set. If it feels like an RPE of 8-10/1-2 reps in reserve? The athlete is done for the day having hit the desired intensity. If it feels like an RPE of 5-7/3-6 RIR? Athletes have the option to add 5-10lbs and complete the plus set for the same number of reps as the third set.

    I find that this increases athlete motivation because they have more autonomy in the training process. I will disallow the plus set if they clearly aren't ready for it, but I will rarely require it and allow them to make that decision based on how they feel. I try my best to create volunteers in the weight room, not hostages, as they are here to play volleyball, not to lift weights.

As far as the training max is concerned, you can either use the Estimated 1RM system I described above to adjust the next week's load, or use the same E1RM from week one to week six. Use what is *practical* in your setting.

2. The next modification I make is in regard to deloads. In Wendler's traditional model, and in many traditional strength and conditioning models, loads increase for three weeks, then the fourth week you back off, or *deload*. This was my typical model at the Division I level, although there was a tremendous amount of fluidity during the competitive season that is outside of the scope of this book.

    However, training middle and high school athletes will organically provide you with frequent deloads, whether you want them or not. In schools, deloads come from:

    - School holidays
    - Field trips
    - Makeup tests and tutorials
    - Standardized testing
    - Missed days due to illness

    After a year of observing "nature's deloads" in the school calendar, I stopped planning formal deloads in my training program. Instead, now I simply modify training on a daily basis using the steak temperature method detailed in Chapter 14. If we are ever in a situation where we're training for 6+ weeks without any break in the action, we'll take a few days or even a week to operate on the

"Rare" end of the spectrum and decrease training load and intensity.

You may have noticed that the 5-3-1 program requires athletes to lift heavier weights, topping out at 95% of their E1RM. Hopefully you didn't read this far into the book and still think:

"Won't lifting heavy weights make volleyball players sore?"

But if you did, the answer is no. There is a far greater risk of incurring soreness by lifting moderate weights for a higher number of reps than from lifting fewer reps with heavier weight, unless the training process has been mangled through inconsistency. If an athlete isn't lifting on a regular basis? Yes, they will get sore. Just like they will get sore from playing volleyball if they haven't been playing volleyball on a regular basis.

Sports follow the same rules that the weight room does:

Inconsistency or doing too much too soon = fatigue and soreness.

Being consistent and properly progressing volume and load = fitness and resiliency.

However, one more time in case you missed it: ***the emphasis is on training athletes, not on putting up big numbers in the weight room.*** There is never a circumstance to risk an athlete's career by compromising technique, no matter how much cooler they may feel having lifted 5 more pounds. Missed reps should be the very rare exception in the weight room, rather than the rule.

NOW THAT YOU'VE READ THIS BOOK, WHAT'S NEXT?!

Start.

The next step is to start writing the program that best fits your specific context, using the principles detailed in this book. Though I've taken the guesswork out of *what* to do, ultimately it is impossible for me to tell every single one of you exactly *how* to do it. Every situation is different and, in the interest of full disclosure, you should understand that there may be a bit of trial and error in figuring out the best way to implement this information given the constraints you face. But let me tell you a secret: after almost 20 years as a strength and conditioning coach, it's a trial and error process for me sometimes too. Each and every time I enter a new setting, things that I could not possibly have planned for inevitably pop up, forcing subtle adjustments to be made to the program.

This is yet another reason I keep my program focused around the basics. That, and the fact that basics work. They work really, really well. And they work for a really, really long time.

And here's another secret: as alluded to throughout the book, there is nothing terribly exciting about the way I've trained any volleyball athletes over the years, even at the Division I level. As I often tell athletes, parents, and coaches:

"I want you to feel underwhelmed by what we do, and I want you to feel overwhelmed by how well we do it."

Execution of the program is the differentiator.

The coach with the fanciest exercises or program rarely develops the best athletes. Instead, it's the coach who plans and executes simple programming on a high level who will see the greatest success. The coach that best adapts this programming to their setting. The coach whose team trains *consistently*.

Using the principles outlined in this book, be that coach. Start writing your program today. Start implementing it tomorrow. And give your developmental athletes the best shot possible at becoming Division I.

ABOUT THE AUTHOR

Missy Mitchell-McBeth has over 20 years of experience in the volleyball strength and conditioning space. She currently serves as the Director of Sports Performance at Fieldhouse Volleyball Club in the DFW metro area where she oversees the athletic development of all top level teams in the 11U through 18U age groups.

Before her time at Fieldhouse, she spent 6 years as the Head Strength and Conditioning Coach at Byron Nelson High School in Trophy Club, Texas. While at Byron, she oversaw the development of 13 different sports and over 500 athletes, including the 2019 UIL 6A State Champion and USA Today #1 Ranked volleyball program.

Prior to Byron Nelson she was the Senior Assistant Strength and Conditioning Coach at TCU in Fort Worth, TX for 7 years. There she handled the development of the Women's Indoor Volleyball, Women's Basketball, and Women's Golf programs.

Before her time as a full-time strength and conditioning professional, Mitchell-McBeth was a High School volleyball coach for 4 years in Copperas Cove, Texas. She holds a Master's degree in Exercise Physiology from Baylor University, and holds SCCC, CSCS, USAW, FRC, and RPR-1 certifications.

She is also the owner of SaFe Iron, a consulting company that teaches sport coaches simplified strength and conditioning systems they can adapt to any environment.

In her free time, Coach Mitchell-McBeth can be found playing beach volleyball.

For more information, follow Missy on Twitter & Instagram **@MissyMMcBeth**, or visit: **MissyMitchellMcBeth.com**

Scan the QR Code or visit **MissyMitchellMcBeth.com/D2D1-Bonus** to access corresponding videos and other exclusive resources:

REFERENCES

Verkhoshansky Y. & Siff M. C. (2009). *Supertraining* (6th ed. - Expanded). Verkhoshansky; Distributed by Ultimate Athlete Concepts.

Bondarchuk, A. (2007) *Transfer of Training in Sports*. Michigan: Ultimate Athlete Concepts.

Lloyd, Rhodri S. PhD, CSCS*D1; Oliver, Jon L. PhD2. *The Youth Physical Development Model: A New Approach to Long-Term Athletic Development*. Strength and Conditioning Journal 34(3):p 61-72, June 2012.

Dechant, Z. (2018). *Movement Over Maxes: Developing the Foundation for Baseball Performance.*

Issurin, V. (2008). *Block Periodization: Breakthrough in Sports Training*. New York, NY: Ultimate Athlete Concepts.

Lauersen JB, Bertelsen DM, Andersen LB. *The effectiveness of exercise interventions to prevent sports injuries: a systematic review and meta-analysis of randomised controlled trials*. Br J Sports Med. 2014 Jun; 48(11):871-7. doi: 10.1136/bjsports-2013-092538. Epub 2013 Oct 7. PMID: 24100287.

McGill, S. (2004) *Ultimate Back Fitness and Performance.* Waterloo, ON: Wabuno Publishers.

Klein K. (1961). *The deep squat exercise as utilized in weight training for athletes and its effects on the ligaments of the knee*. JAPMR. 15(1):6 – 11.

Activcore. (2020, January 8). *Squat Misconception #2: Deep Squats are Bad for the Knees.* Active Core Physical Therapy. https://www.activcore.com/blog/squat-misconception-2-deep-squats-are-bad-for-the-knees

Escamilla, Rafael & MacLeod, Toran & Wilk, Kevin & Paulos, Lonnie & Andrews, James. (2012). *Anterior Cruciate Ligament Strain and Tensile Forces for Weight-Bearing and Non-Weight-Bearing Exercises: A Guide to Exercise Selection.* Journal of Orthopaedic and Sports Physical Therapy. 42. 208-20. 10.2519/jospt.2012.3768.

Escamilla RF. *Knee biomechanics of the dynamic squat exercise.* Med Sci Sports Exerc 33 (1) : 127-141, 2001.

Wu, John & Sinsel, Erik & Carey, Robert & Zheng, Liying & Warren, Christopher & Breloff, Scott. (2019). *Biomechanical modeling of deep squatting: Effects of the interface contact between posterior thigh and shank.* Journal of Biomechanics. 96. 109333. 10.1016/j.jbiomech.2019.109333

Gullett, JC, Tillman, MD, Gutierrez, GM, and Chow, JW. *A biomechanical comparison of back and front squats in healthy trained individuals.* J Strength Cond Res 23: 284–292, 2009.

Young WB, Duthie GM, James LP, Talpey SW, Benton DT, Kilfoyle A. *Gradual vs. Maximal Acceleration: Their Influence on the Prescription of Maximal Speed Sprinting in Team Sport Athletes.* Sports (Basel). 2018 Jul 21;6(3):66. doi: 10.3390/sports6030066. PMID: 30037091; PMCID: PMC6162480.

Friedrich, Tyler. *An alternative way to think about plyometric training for women's volleyball*. Simplifaster. https://simplifaster.com/articles/plyometric-training-womens-volleyball/

Baechle, T. (1989). *Essentials of strength training and conditioning* (4th ed.). Human Kinetics.

Boyle, Michael. (2007, June 20). *A Joint-By-Joint Approach to Training.* T-Nation. https://www.t-nation.com/training/a-joint-by-joint-approach-to-training/

Kenn, J. (2003). *The Coach's Strength Training Playbook: Featuring the Tier System*. Coaches' Choice.

Wendler, J. (2009, July). *5/3/1: How to Build Pure Strength*. T-Nation. https://forums.t-nation.com/t/5-3-1-how-to-build-pure-strength/281694

Made in the USA
Middletown, DE
12 September 2024